Sea Change

Peter Nichols

SEA CHANGE

*Alone Across the Atlantic
in a Wooden Boat*

VIKING

VIKING
Published by the Penguin Group
Penguin Books USA Inc., 375 Hudson Street,
New York, New York 10014, U.S.A.
Penguin Books Ltd, 27 Wrights Lane, London W8 5TZ, England
Penguin Books Australia Ltd, Ringwood, Victoria, Australia
Penguin Books Canada Ltd, 10 Alcorn Avenue,
Toronto, Ontario, Canada M4V 3B2
Penguin Books (N.Z.) Ltd, 182–190 Wairau Road,
Auckland 10, New Zealand

Penguin Books Ltd, Registered Offices:
Harmondsworth, Middlesex, England

First published in 1997 by Viking Penguin,
a division of Penguin Books USA Inc.

10 9 8 7 6 5 4 3 2 1

Page 239 constitutes an extension of this copyright page.

LIBRARY OF CONGRESS CATALOGING IN PUBLICATION DATA
Nichols, Peter, date.
Sea change : alone across the Atlantic in a wooden boat / Peter Nichols.
p.   cm.
ISBN 0-670-87179-6
1. Nichols, Peter, date.—Journeys.   2. Toad (Sailboat).   3. Sailing, Single-handed—
North Atlantic Ocean.   I. Title.
G470.N48   1997
910'.91631—dc21   96-51569

This book is printed on acid-free paper.
∞

Printed in the United States of America
Set in Adobe Perpetua   ·   Designed by Francesca Belanger

For my mother, Barbara Nichols

and my brother and surest friend, David,

who have always understood, and never expected less—or more

For Annie

For my sister Lizzie, and for Matt, Poppy, and Joe

For Poupette

And for Jane

A voyage is a piece of autobiography at best.

—Robert Louis Stevenson, *The Cevennes Journal*

Acknowledgments

I began writing this book at a low point in my life. I'd been writing screenplays and had lost hope that I could ever again write anything that meant something to me. I was low about other things too. The encouragement and support given me during the writing of this book was worth more to me than anyone might have imagined. My brother, David, was the first to read a small portion of it. I came home to a message from him on my answering machine, from India, or Patagonia, where he was producing a movie: "It's wonderful! I loved it! It's the best thing I've ever read! *Fuck* the movies!"—his voice suddenly hoarse with feeling—"This is what you should be doing! Get on with it, mate!" So I did.

Suzanne Gluck at ICM, who has encouraged my writing over a period of many years, next read what I had written and gave me good advice. I am tremendously grateful to Suzanne for putting me in touch with Sloan Harris at ICM, a man who is restoring both an old wooden house and an old wooden boat and thus clearly has a big heart and is able to take great leaps of faith. He became my agent and his strong enthusiasm was worth more to me than he knows. His early and later comments helped shape the book.

Bennett Scheuer, sailor, boatbuilder, reader of great books, read early bits and later drafts. He was my best early sounding board for this book, and helped in many ways. Christine Herrmann, a fine writer, has helped my writing in general and gave me good advice for this book. Peter Birch and Barry Longley praised and savaged, respectively, a first draft with effective results, and I still love Barry—he was right. Mary Louise Rootenberg was a good friend to me while I wrote this book; so also were Judith Tegland, Terri Jaffe, Elly Wood, Pamela Margaux, Judy deMacelli, and Rita Shakin. Dr. Neil Young gave me much help and valuable insight, and some good laughs. Annie Nichols and Jeanne Davis read the first draft and gave me their constructive thoughts. Jeremy Scott and Peter Mayle read later drafts and gave me help I'm grateful for, each in his way. Jeremy continues to provide me with the sort of inspiration to write that no one else could possibly come up with. Susie Watson-Taylor has been a steadfast and generous friend and consistently encouraged my writing. So also has Howard Frumes.

Martin Smith helped me prepare my boat and gave me courage at the beginning of my voyage in *Toad*. I'm grateful to Captain Frank Johnson and his crew of the Lykes Lines' *Almeria Lykes* for their seamanship and assistance. My cousins Matthew deGarmo and Poppy deGarmo gave me two homes at the end of my voyage, and often since, and they and Nancy Gruber, and Chris Fox, gave me the Summer of the Buns.

John Standing—who has also encouraged and promoted my writing over the years—and Annie Cleland both sent me beautiful letters, which contained handsome checks, at the end of *Toad*'s voyage, and their thoughts and hard cash saw me through a difficult period.

My editor at Viking, Carolyn Carlson, has been amazingly enthusiastic from first to last, a good friend, and the tireless and tenacious proponent of a better book than it seemed at times I knew how to write. She saw the forest while I was still lost in the trees, and she helped me chop my way out. I owe her a great debt.

Jane Baldwin read the final draft and made comments that helped me rewrite the last page.

My mother managed to inveigle me to Spain, where she lives, and to keep me there, well-fed from her garden, and undistracted, for much of the writing of this book. And we had the best of times.

Contents

England

June 13

The alarm clock wakes me at six A.M. I turn on the radio for the BBC shipping forecast. Southwesterly gales for sea areas Plymouth and Sole. It was calm and clear six hours ago, when the 0015 forecast made the same prediction. I went to sleep expecting to wake up in a choppy anchorage, hearing gale-force wind in the rigging.

I stick my head out the hatch and look around. The water here in Mylor Creek, a fold in the green hills off the river Fal, in Cornwall, is calm, the sky pale blue and clear except for some high thin cloud. The BBC shipping forecasts often seem full of dire exaggeration. If you wait for a good one you might never leave port. Maybe I should go.

I put on the kettle and get out Alan Watts's slim little book *Instant Weather Forecasting*. Each right-hand page is a color photograph of the sky in some state of meteorological upheaval or transition, the left-hand page a description and table of possibilities. Right now the sky overhead looks very like Photograph 1: "Jet stream cirrus. Sky which means deterioration. A vigorous cyclonic situation exists up-wind and gales may blow up within the next 8–15 hours." That more or less agrees with the BBC. The sky in Photograph 4 also looks quite like what's overhead: "Altostratus ahead of a warm front or occlusion. Sky which means deterioration. If this sky follows that in (1) with cirrostratus (haloes) between, then expect major deterioration."

Right. I'm not leaving today. With such concurrence between Watts and the BBC, I'd be a fool to go to sea, only to realize later on, in the middle of major deterioration, that I could have been ashore at the pub around the hill in Flushing. Yet I still feel cowardly to sit "weatherbound" in port on such a calm, sunny morning. But there is no wind at all right now and I can't go anywhere in my engineless sailboat, *Toad*.

I flip through Watts's book while waiting for the water to boil. Photograph 5 shows low, dark, ragged lumps of cloud, predicting rain or snow within twenty minutes. Photograph 8's thunderstorm cloud is obvious. Photograph 14's "Quiet evening" sky, a bucolic scene with a red sun going down behind farm buildings and a stream of smoke from a small bonfire, makes me wonder why I want to go to sea at all. For a moment I think about not going, but cruising around Britain instead. That was what *Toad* had been built for in 1939, just up the coast, in Paignton, Devon. A day cruiser, a weekender, twenty-seven feet long, with a shallow four-foot draft, built to poke its nose up the Dart or the Fal, wind its way through England's river country, with perhaps, for the truly adventurous, a voyage across the Channel to Brittany, or to Ireland, or up to Scotland and the Western Isles. It was not built to cross oceans, or to live in with a wife and two cats for six years. I have somehow left my wife, J., and the cats, Minou and Neptune, broken up our gypsy home, and am headed across the ocean again, this time alone.

I hope to sell the boat in Maine, on the other side of the Atlantic, where there is a reverence for wooden boats. It has sat here in England for nine months, for sale, listed with a yacht broker, without a single inquiry. The price is not too steep; there is simply no interest. They all want fiberglass boats now. But *Toad* must be sold. It is all J. and I own between us, so it must go.

I'm happy to delay my departure. I still have a few little jobs to do aboard the boat. But mostly I'm scared. I've been real scared, deep down, for a week. Not enough to paralyze me or change my mind, but enough to make sure I'm going to wait for a good forecast and unequivocally benign skies.

My friend Martin has come down from London to stay with me until I leave, to help me prepare the boat and to keep me laughing. After breakfast, we try connecting the light to the new compass I've installed in *Toad*'s cockpit. As soon as I flip the switch we smell burning and the wires immediately melt. We read the wiring instructions now, for the first time. We have to go ashore to buy more wire.

There's wind on the water as we row toward the dock. A popple smacks the dinghy's bow and sends flecks of spray onto my back. I feel better about staying put.

After buying wire in Falmouth and realizing there isn't a lot to do on the boat, Martin and I go sightseeing. We drive to the Lizard, the southernmost of Cornwall's two lobster-claw points, and join a small group climbing through the lighthouse. I want a closer look at Lizard Light, which I steered for coming in from the Atlantic aboard *Toad*, with J., through the long night of an autumn equinoctial gale nine months ago, and whose three-secondly flash will guide me back out to sea again, perhaps tomorrow. I am pulled to lighthouses as much as any postcard photographer because I've spent so many nights at sea looking for them, and seeing their flash at last has always meant joy and relief. Lighthouses sit on rocks or headlands you want to stay clear of, yet you make for them in thick weather in hopes of seeing them to know where you are. Manned lighthouses, a nearly vanished breed, offer the greatest comfort because you know there's someone inside there, experiencing the same weather you are, and you look out at yourself through that person's eyes and wish yourself well.

Inside, Lizard Light is full of brass and neatly painted wood and iron and gunmetal, a snug mix of a ship's fo'c'sle and an English boarding-school dormitory. The giant prismatic lens that revolves on a trough of mercury looks too big, too Jules Verne-ish for the twentieth century. The wind is definitely up now, buffeting the plate-glass windows. Looking out I see the seas building into long white-streaked rollers that come straight in from the southwest horizon and smash onto the base of Lizard Point directly below us. The sailor is always pleased to see such a sight—the more fearful the better—from ashore.

We stop at a pub along Mount's Bay, at Praa Sands, and lunch on Cornish pasties, the old Cornish miner's meat-vegetable-and-potatoes version of calzone, a balanced meal he could shove in his pocket and munch his way through in total darkness. I spent an Easter holiday here at Praa Sands when I was a kid. I shot at birds with my air rifle and saw an adder in the grass above the beach, and took a shy walk along a brambled lane with pretty red-haired Sally Summer, who died of a brain tumor twenty-seven years later; but I don't recognize any of it today. That was Easter 1960, so no wonder. It could be worse. It could look like Cape Cod, where I spent my summers in the 1950s, where it now looks like Los Angeles in places.

We drive on, through piratically motifed Penzance, to Lamorna Cove, where naturalist-author Derek Tangye wrote about his life in a spare, isolated cottage on a cliff, in several books I've read over the winter. Clearly, he was writing when I was playing at Praa Sands, or before. Lamorna Cove is now a place of expensive-looking bungalows hidden behind thick hedges, rosebushes, and Range Rovers.

We head back in driving rain and stop in a warm quayside shack in Marazion, where we drink cups of hot, strong brown tea from an urn and look out at St. Michael's Mount appearing and disappearing in the spume of waves breaking on the quay and clattering over the shack's roof. The weather is thick now, appalling offshore. I feel intensely happy to be looking smugly out at it while driving between pubs and cafés.

Back aboard *Toad*, we replace the wire and connect the compass light. We take turns going out into the cockpit to marvel at the illuminated compass, while the other flicks the switch on and off several times.

"God, I wish the fuck I was coming with you," says Martin.

At seven P.M., the sky—looking much like Photograph 6, "A front passes"—brightens and the rain stops. June at 50 degrees north means it will stay light until almost eleven P.M. We row ashore again and take the footpath around a hill of pasture and rich dark cowpats to the pub in Flushing, a village across the Penryn River from Falmouth, where we play billiards and eat bacon, eggs, and chips for dinner.

Toad spent the winter on a mooring off Flushing, and on a nice day this spring when my brother, David, and I tried to sail her around the hill to Mylor, we strayed out of the unmarked channel and ran aground on a falling tide directly in front of this pub. We threw out the anchor and rowed ashore to have ploughman's lunches and a pint and wait for the tide to change. As we sat at the bar gazing out the window at a boat we both loved lying on its side in the mud at an awkward angle, the publican made a humorous but slightly derisive remark about fair-weather sailors running aground. David, who had sailed aboard *Toad* in the Caribbean and in the Mediterranean, bristled. He asked the publican if no one else ever went aground there. Not often, was the smirking reply. We drank up and went outside.

"That little boat right there," David yelled outside the pub, "has been more places than that asshole has had hot dinners! I'd like to see him take that boat where it's gone! Without a fucking engine!" And we walked on along the footpath into Falmouth to find another pub, while David yelled, "Asshole! Jerk!"

Martin has also spent happy weeks aboard *Toad*, in the Bahamas and the Mediterranean, and has heard all about this episode. As we play billiards in the Flushing pub (which is convenient to the boat-yard in Mylor, and all that a salty shoreside pub should be), he looks across the room every now and then at the publican and mutters, "Asshole."

At midnight, I am again lying in my bunk in the dark, listening to BBC Radio 4, waiting for the 0015 forecast. You tune in to a different world when you listen to the shipping forecast: a gray, blue, green, clear and foggy, calm and storm-swept nation of twenty-eight contiguous sea areas surrounding the British Isles, reaching almost as far north as Iceland ("Southeast Iceland") and down to northern Spain and Portugal ("Finisterre"). Few Britons, planning voyages to the High Street shops, wanting only to know if they need to take along a mac or a brolly, will be bothered by the information that the wind in Viking, Forties, Dogger, and German Bight will be blowing gale-force eight to storm-force nine imminently. But to the poor buggers at sea in those areas, listening to the radio as if waiting to hear a judgment, this will be grim news. To them it means everything. It means danger off-loading men and cargo on a storm swell beneath an oil rig; it means the possibility of steel hawsers and chains snapping and whiplashing through a trawler crew. In a yacht (where you find yourself by choice, either as crew or owner; and if you're the owner, you've spent a lot of money to get there) it means long hours of questioning what it is exactly you're getting out of this sport. For all who hear a gale forecast at sea, it means life reduced to a concentrated attempt to survive. They will envy the BBC announcer, sitting in a warm studio atop a concrete foundation (I always imagine him wearing a Marks and Spencer cardigan, a cup of cocoa at hand), reading this forecast in his rich, plummy voice, after which he will drive home to Surbiton or Clapham or Barnes in a warm car and go to bed. They will long to be ashore, close to their families, at home in bed. Nothing on earth will get them there before the forecasted weather arrives. They can make no deal to avoid it. They will have to see it through. There is just one thing they can do that might make a difference: they can pray. No wonder mariners are God-fearing.

There is no bad weather forecast tonight. No mention of the gales that have blown earlier today. The wind in sea areas Plymouth and Sole—where I am and where I'm going—is forecast to veer to the west and northwest and drop from Beaufort force 6 to 4 (twenty-two to twenty-seven knots to eleven to sixteen knots).

This is unsettling news. It means I might have to go tomorrow.

June 14

Six hours later, the forecast is the same, better even: the wind is predicted to drop to force 3 or 4, or seven to sixteen knots. The sky outside is clear.

I call John, on *Corrinna*, anchored off Penryn, on *Toad*'s VHF radio. He's watching the weather also, waiting to head out for Portugal and the Med. He says it's a good forecast for him, heading southwest for Brittany; it puts the northwesterly wind on his beam, a nice reach. He'll be off, he says, as soon as he tops up his fuel tanks. I tell him I'll probably go too, and we say good-bye and wish each other good trips. It's all right for him. *Corrinna* is a fifty-foot-long ferro-cement ketch, with a fifty-horse diesel in her. John could push her through the Antarctic Ice Pack if he wanted to.

I decide to go—there's no good reason to stay.

Martin and I clean up the boat, and he packs his bag. I go forward once more and work my way aft through the boat, checking that all is stowed properly.

In the forepeak is my double bunk, which I won't use once at sea, covered now with bags of clothes, spare line, spare lots of things. Up here, in a tiny cubicle, is also the head, where my foul-weather gear hangs on hooks, and a string bag holds a three-month stash of toilet paper and paper towels.

Coming aft I enter the saloon: a bunk down each side, lockers filled with food forming backrests, and above the lockers, shelves crammed with books held against the hull with wooden fiddles and shock cord. Beneath the bunks on both sides are fiberglass water tanks I built, holding together almost ninety gallons. Coming down through the middle of the boat, from deck to keel, up between the two forward bulkheads, is an octagonal piece of Scottish pine, eight inches in diameter. This supports the mast, which is actually stepped on the deck above, in a tabernacle—a hinge that enables it to be lowered without lifting it out of the boat. Aft of this mast support, running three feet down through the middle of the saloon, is a gimballed teak dropleaf table, on which I can leave a cup of coffee or plate of food in all but the worst weather. A kerosene Aladdin lamp is held by a small braided line over the forward end of the table. This is the main light aboard the boat, the light I read by. On the forward bulkheads (the partitions between the saloon and forward cabin) are screwed *Toad*'s brass clock and barometer, on which hang a shell necklace and a whalebone marlinspike on a piece of leather; a magazine rack full of *National Geographic*, *The New Yorker*, and *WoodenBoat* magazines; and a large framed Paul Davis print of two fish on a beach with storm clouds gathering out at sea. Stuck into the frame are photographs of J. and one of my dead father playing his clarinet, his eyes closed, eyebrows raised, his face contorted like Eric Clapton's. On the aft saloon bulkhead, to starboard, is a solid-fuel heating stove, inside which I keep my money and my passport; to port is an elegant teak cabinet holding glasses, mugs, and spare wicks for the Aladdin lamp.

Aft of the saloon is the galley, to starboard, with a gimballed three-burner propane stove with grill and oven, a long counter spanning the full eight-foot width of the boat, with a sink sunk into it, and more books filling a recess behind the counter. In racks on the galley bulkhead are plates and cutlery. Huge lockers beneath the counter are filled with pots and pans and baking dishes. A small, gimballed brass kerosene lamp is fixed to the galley bulkhead over the stove.

To port, opposite, is the chart table. More books, mostly pilot and navigational volumes, sit at its edge held against the hull with shock cord. Beneath the chart table are my charts, about a hundred, collected over the years, mildewed, discolored, and stained, a big part of what I think of as my personal wealth. Beneath the chart space are lockers for my sextant and any other gear that has to do with the management of the boat. On the bulkhead over the chart table is a teak box holding binoculars, flashlight, handbearing compass. A kerosene hurricane lamp (which tends to blow out in winds stronger then twenty-five knots) hangs from a hook over the chart table and it bumps into my head all the time.

Toad does not have an engine. It did once, and its former owner threw it overboard when it conked out. J. and I never had enough money to put another one in, and without question I would love to have an engine. But in the space aft of the galley and chart table, where the engine and all its nasty tanks and business would have been, is an enormous clean, well-painted storage space, holding jugs of kerosene for my lighting, spare lumber for emergency ship-building, tools, more food, spare anchors, chain, rope, paint, varnish, boxes of screws, bolts, shackles, spare parts for the galley water pump, the bilge pump, the head, spares for everything I can think of.

Everything looks tidy and secure below. I climb up into the cockpit.

On deck, *Toad* is clean and spare and rigged for sea. The only thing not bolted down as part of the rigging and running rigging is the fiberglass dinghy, turned upside down and lashed to ring-bolts that go down through the cabin roof and its oak beams, and the dinghy's mast and oars, which are tied to the handrails along the cabin roof.

All looks shipshape aboard *Toad*.

We raise the anchor and tack up to the fuel dock. We fill the water tanks and hose off the boat. We have a ploughman's lunch in the cockpit: bread, cheddar cheese, and Branston Pickle (a chunky English relish, the indispensable ingredient of the ploughman's lunch) from one of two jars that I hope will last me the trip. I watch Martin and hope he doesn't use too much, but I won't say anything. In fact, he says he doesn't want to use any of my stores, and I say, "Don't be silly, go ahead, it's just relish."

The wind doesn't drop, though. Throughout the afternoon it remains strong, at least twenty to twenty-five knots. Heading west-southwest, it will be forward of *Toad*'s beam, an uncomfortable point of sail for my somewhat tubby boat, an "inefficient" design according to modern trends. It could force me down toward Brittany, and the rocks and tide rips around Île de Ouessant, where, without an engine, calm conditions could be even worse than strong winds. It isn't what I want to start with. I want, unreasonably, completely favorable conditions. But the sky is blue; I know the wind will go down later in the evening. I should go.

I open my logbook (loose pages in a ring binder) and write:

Log of Yacht TOAD, from Mylor, Cornwall, England to—hopefully— Camden, Maine, via Horta, Fayal, Azores.

I turn the page and write:

At anchor, Mylor. Decided to go. But now—1730—am very chicken. Wind still quite strong. Am feeling all the usual predeparture feelings— fear, loneliness, and a great desire to buy a farm—if I could afford one— but very much more so now without J.

Normal feelings, healthy even. To be unafraid when setting out to sea is unintelligent. The dangers are clear and to be aware of them is to be prepared for them. Eric Hiscock, the English yachtsman and writer of sailing books, whose complete oeuvre I have read and reread many times and carry aboard *Toad*, wrote:

Although the commencement of a long voyage in a small sailing vessel is not yet an everyday happening [it is now—Hiscock was writing in 1967], it is not uncommon, and I sometimes wonder if the people concerned suffer from similar feelings to mine on such occasions: tense apprehension because of the knowledge that we will be dependent entirely on our own skill and resources, and a sad empty feeling at leaving behind the people and the things we love. I had hoped, as the years went by and I gained experience and a little more confidence in myself, that such feelings might become less strong; but I found on this departure in late June . . . that I was just as apprehensive and just as sad as ever I had been before.

And Eric had Susan Hiscock with him, the woman who never let a day go by in forty years of circumnavigating, whatever the weather, when she didn't give Eric a hot meal, whistling as she prepared it. (However, Eric always did the dishes.) Susan also navigated, and handled their boat as well as Eric. Although he wrote the books, she matched him in every sailorly endeavor, and he handsomely acknowledged her contribution at the very beginning of *Around the World in Wanderer III*, the book covering their first circumnavigation, when he wrote that she was the true heroine of the story.

Another sailor-author, Miles Smeeton, who sailed around the world with his extraordinarily adventure-driven wife, Beryl, wrote this about people going to sea alone:

> When they are tired there is no one to take their watch, when they are anxious there is no one to relieve them of their anxiety, when they think they are sick there is no one to laugh them out of it, when they are fearful there is no one to lend them courage, when they are undetermined there is no one to harden their resolve, and when they are cold there is no one to hand them a warm drink.

I'm going alone now. I've done almost all my sailing, so far, with J., who whistled too, which was always nice to hear when I was below on a dark night and she was on watch in the cockpit, and she handed me warm drinks, and gave me courage. To think of going to sea without her seems impossible. And disloyal.

We bought *Toad* for $6,000 in the Virgin Islands a year after we were married. We remained in the Virgins for almost three years, living aboard the boat while we slowly rebuilt it. I worked as a charter boat skipper, taking pale yuppies out on other boats, "bare-boats," for a week at a time. Often, space permitting, I took J. with me. From St. Thomas, the base for the charter companies I worked for, we zigzagged up through the islands—Jost Van Dyke, Tortola, Peter Island, Virgin Gorda—and back, stopping at every beautiful beach and cove in between. Dinner was speared fish or crayfish, or the "gourmet" meals packed into the boat's icebox, or the cheeseburger in paradise ashore. "You're *paid* to do this!" my charterers never failed to tell me. They marveled at the life J. and I were leading on our "cute little boat" and bemoaned going back to their jobs and mortgages.

We lived very simply, more simply than I think they understood or would care to try themselves, despite the way they'd rave on about envying our lifestyle. Living at anchor, we had no bills. We had no electricity. No refrigerator or TV. At night we read by the light of kerosene lamps and listened to the radio. Our dinghy was our car. Ashore we walked or took buses. We lived hand to mouth, but our only expenses were our food and the boat. I took skippering jobs as we needed the money. The rest of the time we sailed *Toad* or worked on turning it into as livable and good a boat as we could make it. We made plans to sail around the world. In the meantime we sailed around the Virgin Islands, and once to St. Barts when David visited us. Finally we did sail away, to Puerto Rico and the Dominican Republic, up through the Bahamas to Florida, where we stayed for eighteen months. Then across the Atlantic by way of Bermuda and the Azores to the Mediterranean, and then to England, where all our plans foundered and we broke up.

It seems a wonderful life when I look back on it like this, as if through a photo album, seeing the pictures. I remember the unpleasant episodes too, but now, set against the bigger picture of our life aboard *Toad*, they seem inconsequential. I keep thinking there must surely have been much more wrong with us than I can remember. Deeply and seriously wrong, to have thrown all that away. And now, for the first time, I'm going somewhere aboard *Toad* without her. I'm not sure how I'm going to do it.

"Fuck it. Go tomorrow," says Martin, with great pith. He has been quiet and businesslike all day as we've prepared the boat. We've been best friends since we were both twelve, despite rather than because he is also J.'s brother. We met in Mallorca, where my parents owned a house and we spent our summers, and where Martin and J.'s French mother lived after she had left them and their father and run off with a Mallorquín tennis pro while they were vacationing at the Hotel Formentor one summer. She stayed in Mallorca when their father took them back to the States. Martin and J. spent most summers with her after that.

J. was ten when I first saw her on a dusty unpaved street in Cala Ratjada, a skinny American kid with white-blond hair walking with a dark little Mallorquín girl, both yakking away in Spanish. When I got to know her after running around with Martin all summer, I found her alternately taciturn and wildly mischievous, disconcertingly sharp and acerbic. She was not intimidated by two older, boorish twelve-year-olds. If we messed with her she could make us—or me, anyway—feel very small. She was a pain and I was fascinated by her. As we grew into our teens, seeing each other only in the summers, we kept a wary eye on each other. She hung out with French and Spanish boys, while I hung out with their sisters. There was something between us that we wouldn't touch, like a secret we both knew was there without knowing what it was. Then we didn't see each other for years. We met again in our early twenties. Martin had married and we all got together and went skiing for a few days in Switzerland. I was stupidly amazed to find J. had become a woman, lithe, beautiful, with wonderful tawny thick blond hair. And deflatingly bright, more disconcerting, more unpredictable. We were still wary of each other, careful of how we proceeded, as if touching something awfully big, so we still didn't touch it. A few more years went by. I heard through Martin that she had met a

Bolivian and gone to Bolivia. Then, at the end of one summer, I found myself in Mallorca again after eight weeks working as crew on an eighty-foot yacht sailing around the Mediterranean, and J. was there too, looking sensational and exotic in Levi's and Cochabamba casual wear, visiting her mother. Her boyfriend, José, had gone back to Bolivia temporarily, although they were still in touch and planning to see each other again. I was twenty-six and J. was twenty-four, and I finally realized I was in love with her. I asked her to marry me. I wooed her, persuaded her that we had always been meant for each other, that there was no one else for either of us. I appealed to that part of her that was also in me that thought our history pointed this way, that this was unavoidably true. I was relentless, I was so sure, I was convincing. A few months later we were married in England.

Martin has watched us grow up, circle each other like two cats, get married, and sail off together. He's sailed with us, and he's seen us break up. His emotions at now seeing me sail off alone are probably as full and complex as mine.

"Go tomorrow," he says again. "The weather'll be better. I want to play some more billiards. And we've still got to check out that point."

"Okay."

We have dinner at the pub in Flushing again and play more billiards. Afterward, at ten o'clock, when it's just beginning to get dark, we drive to Pendennis Point, the promontory at the entrance to Falmouth's harbor. Martin is going to drive here when I leave and take pictures of *Toad* as I sail past. We find a good spot for him, low down on the rocks near the water. I will steer for this spot tomorrow, and he will be waiting, camera ready.

Falmouth to Fayal

June 15

From my log:

0625 forecast: Plymouth: Northwesterly winds 5–6, decreasing 3–4; Sole: Variable winds, 3 or less. Decided (again) to leave. Looks real good: wind Northwest (but may just be funneling effect down Mylor Creek). Sunny day. Barometer very high. I'm feeling much better. Called Ma and said goodbye. Now 1125, about to leave.

Toad is again alongside the dock, facing the wind.

Standing on the dock with Martin, watching me prepare to take off, is Wilfred, another yachtie who lives on a small boat anchored in Mylor Creek. Wilfred is of indeterminate middle age and looks like a schoolteacher who has been living in a car for some time. His unvarying costume, week after week, is a threadbare houndstooth jacket, dark gray polyester trousers that are shiny and oily brown with wear and grime, and black shoes rotting from repeated immersion in the water in the bottom of his dinghy as he rows ashore. Underneath the jacket the same gray wool turtleneck sweater. He wears black National Health glasses, which he has broken and is continually and unsuccessfully trying to jury-rig with epoxy, seizing wire, small screws, and Swan Vesta matchstick splints. His only nautical concession is a blue wool watchcap I've never seen him take off. While *Toad* was hauled out on the hard in Mylor's boatyard for three weeks, Wilfred came and stood beside me every day and relentlessly told me the details of his grim personal life while I rebuilt the wind vane, slapped on bottom paint, and generally made ready for sea. He and his wife fell out. He's been living aboard his boat for six months. He's fixing it up to sail to the Caribbean. I've seen his boat, a small, sad bilge keeler, in much the same shape as his glasses.

We've had a few pints together at the pub around the hill. Wilfred feels he and I have much in common, with our little boats, our estranged wives, our dreams of leaving. He gives me the willies: he is what I hope I don't turn into. I feel he is not a long way from the homeless man whose major preoccupation is fixing up his shopping cart. But I've detected no desperation in Wilfred. He seems perfectly happy.

I say a heartfelt good-bye to him. He seems a little amazed that I'm really going. He asks me to send him a postcard from the Azores.

Martin and I hug and I step aboard. I raise the mainsail and jib, leaving their sheets slack, the sails flapping. Martin casts off the two shore lines and throws them aboard, while I stand on the foredeck and back the jib, holding its clew out to port. The wind fills the sail and pushes *Toad*'s bow off the dock. *Toad* and I drift slowly away from the shore. It's exactly noon.

"You better get going," I say to Martin, who is still almost arm's length away and now shooting pictures like a paparazzo. "I'm going as the crow flies, but you've got to get through Falmouth at lunchtime. And I'm not waiting."

He heads for the car. I steer the boat for Carrick Roads, the Fal's wide channel that lies beyond the hill Martin and I walked around to reach the pub in Flushing.

Farther out in the creek, I jibe *Toad*, bringing the wind onto our starboard quarter. I slip the quarter-inch stainless steel bolt that hangs on the end of a piece of string into the holes on my home-made self-steering gear, connecting the wind vane to the trim-tab on the rudder, and the boat begins, magically, to steer itself. I go forward and stand on the foredeck and look around like a sightseer as *Toad* takes us down the river toward the sea.

At 1230, we're approaching Pendennis Point. I can see Martin waving and taking pictures. I go aft and alter the vane setting and head us close in. As we pass him, he starts shouting. "Wait! God-

dammit!" He's frantically going through a bag. "I've got to put another roll in!" He's shot too many pictures too fast and now that we're approaching perfect range, he's out of film.

"You idiot!" I shout back. "No way!" I have a good wind, not strong, but it's behind me, well slanted to get me clear of land, and I'm not going to waste a second of it. I have the tide too, and I quickly leave Martin behind, on his knees on the rocks, trying to load his camera, his shouts—"Goddammit it! *Fuck iiiiiiit!*"—fading fast. I wave. He remains there for as long as I can see him, until he becomes an indistinguishable dot against the town of Falmouth. And I know just how he feels as he watches me and *Toad* for as long as he can as we shrink into a bobbing dot with a stick on it heading out to sea.

We pass Black Rock in the middle of the harbor entrance and I think of sailor-mountaineer H. W. "Bill" Tilman, who, sailing from Falmouth on July 6, 1955, bound for the Straits of Magellan aboard his pilot cutter *Mischief* was becalmed right here:

> We passed Black Rock, and the sentiments appropriate to watching from the deck of a small ship, outward bound on a long voyage, the receding shores of one's native land, had barely found expression when the shores ceased to recede. The wind which had hitherto been light now failed altogether and for two hours we drifted off the headland of St Anthony viewing its not remarkable features from many different angles.

I have Tilman's wonderful, dry book, *Mischief in Patagonia*, aboard, along with my Hiscocks and many other narratives of cruises in small boats. These books are, for me, the finest of company. When your course converges with a cruise covered by one of these books, its author seems to come along with you. And you join that group of sailors that has gone before you.

I don't have to look at St. Anthony's not remarkable head from many angles as Tilman did. It's at the far side of Falmouth Bay and quickly behind me as I head now for the lightbuoy off a group of rocks called The Manacles 6 miles ahead, and beyond that, Lizard Point and its light, 15 miles distant.

I stream the Walker log—my nautical odometer: a small torpedo-shaped propeller on a line attached to a dial on the boat's transom—change the jib to a genoa, and make myself a peanut butter and jelly sandwich. I've made the mistake of getting my peanut butter where I got all my beans for the trip, at Neal's Yard, the stylish and irreproachably holistic health food store in London. Like all health-food-store peanut butter, it has the consistency of mortar almost gone-off, with separated oil requiring long minutes of stiff, spoon-bending mixing before it's spreadable. As I sit in the cockpit eating my sandwich in nice weather, watching the English coast float smoothly by, I realize my fear and apprehension have subsided to a small, manageable little pulse somewhere deep down, and my only regret is that I haven't bought Skippy.

At four P.M. Lizard Light, where Martin and I were tourists two days ago, is well in view, two and a half miles north-northwest. I look at it through my binoculars. I wouldn't have gone there, or had tea in the shack on the rainy quay at Marazion, or played billiards in the pub, without Martin. I'd have stayed in Mylor, frightened and lonely, working on the boat until it was time to go, and then gone, with only Wilfred to see me off. I miss Martin now.

The long sweep of Mount's Bay, with Praa Sands and Lamorna Cove, slides into view as we pass the Lizard; Land's End, Cornwall's southwesternmost lobster claw, is visible at the far end.

The late afternoon forecast is for light and variable winds in sea areas Plymouth and Sole. The tide turns against us in the early evening and we move slowly away from the land through the long northern twilight.

2130. Slipping along nicely, doing about 3 1/2 knots. Wolf Rock, Lizard, and Land's End lights all in view and flashing, though it's still not dark.

2200. Wind has veered northeasterly, very good for us. Staysail down, main and genoa poled out wing-and-wing.

2330. Almost becalmed. Stars out now. Lovely night, and I'm grateful that it's an easy and peaceful one.

June 16

My sailor's day begins at midnight. I turn a page in my logbook and write, on the right-hand page: "June 16. Day 2." On this page I write my comments, which, depending on conditions and my state of mind, can be straightforward comments on what's going on, long chatty riffs, or short, nearly illegible, salt-stained scrawls giving basic navigational information. I divide the left-hand page into six columns, headed *Time, Course, Wind, Force, Log, Barometer.* Now at midnight I fill them in: 0000, 270, NE, 1–2, 35, 1041.

The 0015 forecast states that a high-pressure area has become stationary to the west of Ireland. Winds in areas Plymouth and Sole are predicted to be northerly, becoming variable, force 3–4 or less. The wind is revolving around the high in a clockwise direction, interrupting the pattern of prevailing westerlies that would have had me beating to windward in lumpy seas, making slow progress. I'm sneaking away to the southwest on the high's eastern edge, and the light northerlies will gradually become easterly the farther west I move, as long as the high remains where it is. I hope it does.

I begin to feel sleepy. At 0130 I set my alarm clock for 0145 and lie down on a saloon bunk. Ten minutes later I'm still awake and too anxious to wait for the alarm. I get up and climb halfway out of the hatch and look around. The vane is holding *Toad* on course. The lighthouses are flashing. There are no ship lights, at this moment, although we're just outside the traffic separation zone for all shipping coming in and out of the English Channel. There may still be all sorts of boats—fishing vessels, yachts, submarines—anywhere in the waters around me (my chart for Cornwall and the Isles of Scilly notes: "Submarines exercise frequently, both surfaced and dived, in the area covered by this chart. A good lookout is to be kept for them when passing through these waters")—but I see no lights.

I go below, set the alarm for fifteen minutes hence, and lie down once more. Again, though beginning to relax, I remain awake, finally unable to wait for the alarm before getting up to look around.

The third time it all catches up with me: days of anxiety, final departure, the late hour. For the first time, I manage to fall fast asleep while alone at sea.

Rule 5 of the International Regulations for Preventing Collisions at Sea, known as COLREGS, requires that "every vessel shall at all times maintain a proper lookout by sight and hearing as well as by all available means appropriate in the prevailing circumstances and conditions so as to make a full appraisal of the situation and of the risk of collision."

Clearly, someone sailing alone can't do this. After more than a day or two at sea, the singlehander will grow tired and go to sleep, and the boat, hopefully maintaining its course by means of some self-steering arrangement, will continue on, illegally and blindly. Despite the wide publicity given to many singlehanded voyages and high-profile singlehanded races, no authority has yet come down the dock to ticket or arrest a singlehander for noncompliance with COLREGS Rule 5. But the inability to keep watch at all times is a life-threatening risk the singlehander has to come to terms with.

All sorts of junk and debris litter the oceans of the world, waterlogged, mostly submerged, and usually impossible to see until it's too late to alter course: heavy logs, oil drums, and, probably most catastrophic of all if a yacht should hit one, containers that have fallen off container ships. You hear rumors about containers and read such rumors in the yachting press. A container would be a floating reef, lethal enough to wreck almost any yacht. Tightly shut and packed with sofas, antiques, mail, food, bicycles, and computers, a container could remain afloat for days, even weeks. A number of yachts in recent years have been holed and sunk after colliding with "an unknown object." A container, maybe. Then there are whales, asleep or otherwise. A few yachts have been sunk by whales, and these incidents are well recorded by the survivors, who typically have spent weeks in rubber rafts and later appear in yachting magazines endorsing pocket-sized reverse-osmosis water-makers. And, rarely, there are yachts that leave port and are never heard from again, their crews lost at sea for unknown reasons. But the number of sinkings, from whales or unknown objects, is still small compared with the thousands of successful voyagers crossing oceans, sailing all over the world, alone or with a mate. And if you do collide with some such object, you're as likely as not to hit it at a glancing angle, making a thud loud enough to give you a heart attack, and sail on with little or no damage, not even knowing what it was.

I believe the greatest risk facing the singlehander while asleep below is being run down by a ship.

Until the last thirty years or so, most ships kept to well-defined shipping lanes, routes across oceans that offered the most favorable combination of weather, ocean conditions, and distance. The British Admiralty publication *Ocean Passages of the World*, a pilot book detailing these preferred routes for high- and low-powered vessels, as well as for sailing vessels, still comes with a chart showing these shipping lanes. Early singlehanders—and the sleepy shorthanded crews of other small sailboats—could avoid these highways in the sea, or, if they had to cross or approach shipping lanes, knew what to expect and could remain awake or catnap for a few days. Afterward, out of harm's way, they could, and usually did, turn in for hours at a time.

Then ships began to stray out of their lanes. They became more powerful, able to head more directly for their destinations against prevailing winds and currents. They began to get daily meteorological faxes and radio reports from shore stations giving them optimum courses around local weather systems. Soon they were all over the oceans, and the singlehander could run into and be run down by a ship anywhere.

At one time, the singlehander under sail could hope that the approaching ship would see him and alter course—as it is legally obliged to do: a vessel under sail has right-of-way over an engine-driven ship. In Eric Hiscock's early books, recounting voyages made in the thirties, forties, and fifties, he and Susan would hang a kerosene lamp in the cockpit and go below for a good night's sleep, trusting that any oncoming vessel would have a man in the bow peering out into the dark ahead, who would see their little light and send a message back to the bridge and the ship would turn away. That halcyon world—when ships were not only well manned but also beautiful, and old orange peel was the only pollution you might see floating in the ocean—is, of course, gone. Now there is probably no one looking out from the bow. As ships have grown larger and their systems more sophisticated, manpower aboard has been cut back. A supertanker may have less than twenty men aboard, and at any given time a third of that complement will be off duty, asleep or watching Rambo videos in the saloon. A few shipping lines still maintain a good lookout, posting a man on the bow in radio contact with the bridge. Other ships, particularly those registered under the less demanding requirements of flags of convenience, are not so scrupulous. Lookout may be by radar alone, and if the radar doesn't pick you up, you're invisible. Yachts, particularly wooden yachts, do not make good radar pictures. They're small, their radar echoes may be lost in "sea clutter"—you may look like just another wave on the radar screen. And the radar, as I've often found when calling a ship by VHF radio to ask what sort of radar picture my boat made, may be turned off.

The bridge of a large tanker may be a quarter of a mile astern of its bow and a hundred and fifty feet above the water—something like the view from the upper floors of a condo on Miami Beach looking out at the Florida Straits. The crew on the bridge can see the big stuff, other ships, from up there, but little sailboats can go unnoticed. At night, a sailboat's navigation lights, close down to the water, will almost certainly not be seen farther than half a mile away, even if anyone's looking—scant minutes to collision. Then, if seen, the maneuverability of a large ship is poor and slow.

Undoubtedly, it's up to the dinky sailboat to stay clear of the ship. You have to see it, first, then you have to watch it to determine its course, and finally you may have to alter your course to avoid it, speeding out of its path at four knots per hour. If you don't have an engine, you better hope the wind is blowing.

Then there is this: The curve of the earth, you quickly realize when you go to sea, is quite pronounced. The horizon seen from the deck of a small yacht circles you at a distance of about three miles. Beyond three miles, a ship will be "hull-down" below the horizon, only its superstructure visible. Eight miles away, the whole ship will be below the horizon. Conditions of haze, cloud, rain, fog, or a large swell on a sunny day can reduce this to yards. A ship moving at eighteen knots (the speed at which the average container ship might travel—many travel faster), unseen when you come on deck and make your periodic scan of sea around you and then go below again, can steam up over the horizon and run you down in twenty minutes or less.

This last winter I bought and read John S. Letcher, Jr.'s book *Self Steering for Sailing Craft*, and made some improvement to *Toad*'s homemade wind vane. Letcher, who has a Ph.D. in aeronautics and applied mathematics from the California Institute of Technology, and has sailed more than 25,000 miles in his own small, homemade engineless sailboats in both the Atlantic and Pacific, also wrote about the risk of collision in his book:

> For a quantitative estimate of the risks from merchant shipping on a particular passage, find out approximately how many ships will cross your projected track during the expected duration of the passage. These statistics are available from port authorities, and are compiled in the U.S. Bureau of the Census publication FT975, "Vessel Entrances and Clearances", and in Lloyd's Register of Shipping, Statistical Tables.

First, consider just one of these ships. It will have to pass (on center) within about 50 feet on either side of you to make contact; so there is a section of your track only 100 feet long that is endangered by this ship. If the ship crosses at a random line, the probability that you are in the section is just 100 feet divided by length of passage. This risk is multiplied by the total number of ships crossing, to give the probability of a collision *if neither party ever looks out*.

Example: On a passage from Hawaii to Alaska (2,500 miles) I expected to take 30 days and I obtained an estimate of five ships per day, on the average, arriving or departing west coast ports for the Orient. This makes 150 ships crossing my track. The probability of collision is

$$(150 \times 100 \text{ ft}) \div (2500 \text{ mi} \times 6080 \text{ ft/mi}) = 1 \div 1012$$

This can be reduced, of course, by several measures on both vessels' parts. But even so it says I could sail blind back and forth continuously across these waters and expect to be run down only once in a thousand voyages—over 80 years of continuous sailing.

These calculations initially assuaged any fear Letcher had of collision, enabling him to spend whole nights in his bunk: "I used to delight in waking up . . . listen a moment to the familiar symphony of sounds from spars, rigging, sails, and the water rushing past, and then drift back to sleep."

Then, returning to California from Alaska in 1965:

That night I saw the lights of many ships, one or two per hour, passing a little way inshore. We were running under twins, but by midnight the wind had almost died and progress—and maneuverability—had become very poor. One northbound ship appeared for a long while as if it were going to pass a little outside us, but rather close. I assumed they were seeing my lights, and was a little annoyed that they would pass so close. As their lights drew closer, and the muffled whine of turbines and the rush of the bow wave came across the water to me, I turned on my searchlight and aimed it at the ship. This was just to let them know I was annoyed. Imagine my horror when the ship turned and came directly toward me! White over white, red beside green, the group of lights approached with an awful noise, growing by the second, and there was not the slightest chance of getting out of its path. As the pale bow loomed out of the darkness I dived through the companionway and instantly there was a terrible jolt and a rending crash. In a few seconds of shuddering vibration the ship's side rushed past. . . . They never knew we were there. . . . It turned out there was no contact between our hulls . . . their bow wave washed *Island Girl*'s hull aside, but her rig rolled into the side of the ship. The mast was broken in three places, the forestay, headstay, and bowsprit were all broken, and the upward pull of the forestay lifted the deck and clamps so the sheer strakes were split almost back to the chain plates. I got away with my life and felt very lucky.

In 1969, Letcher, this time with his wife Pati aboard, was again returning to California from Alaska. They were north of San Francisco, well clear of shipping lanes:

Pati awoke to the sound of an engine approaching. On looking out she saw . . . a fishing boat about to cut us in two! Her desperate yell brought me out of my bunk, sleeping bag and all, and when I saw this boat through the portlight I yelled too. Pati was trying to unlash the helm and start the mainsheet, but before she could do either, the fishing boat struck us a cruel blow on the lee quarter . . . if he had hit us dead center I don't think we'd be alive. We raised Cain, blowing the horn and yelling until the boat was a mile away, but he kept straight on, evidently on autopilot, and we never saw anyone on board.

Sailing alone or with his wife, Letcher thereafter kept a regular lookout.

To try to avoid this sort of thing, the singlehander only sleeps for short periods. You have to wake yourself up and climb out of your bunk and look around every fifteen, twenty, thirty minutes—there's no rule, it varies from singlehander to singlehander. I've met people who sleep for an hour or more between lookouts. You sleep as long as you dare, according to your temperament. You guess, viscerally, at the sort of odds Letcher so carefully calculated. You rationalize that it would be unlikely and unlucky indeed for a ship, unseen when you last looked out, to come along and meet you in one tiny spot on all the open ocean around you in the period before you next stick your head up through the hatch and look around. But after you've altered course a few times to try to get away from a ship that seems to be coming too close, you begin to see how amazingly unlucky you can be.

At night, when J. and I sailed together, one of us had always been "on watch." On *Toad*, with the wind vane doing most of the steering, this usually meant relaxing below, reading, writing, cooking, listening to the radio, and sticking our heads out the companionway hatch every fifteen minutes for a careful look around. The other would be asleep. Depending on conditions and how we felt, our watches usually lasted about four hours. Then we'd wake the other up. Getting enough sleep had rarely been a problem.

Now that I'm alone, I've decided that while I'm at sea between England and the U.S. coast, I'm not going to let myself sleep longer than thirty minutes at a stretch. Here, close to land or shipping, I'll make that fifteen minutes. I've never slept like this before, but I've read about other singlehanders doing it, so I will do it.

For this trip, I have bought a new alarm clock. I've taken some care choosing it. It's a Casio, powered by two AA batteries. It is white, small, easily stashed on the bookshelves above the saloon bunks, but it has large, easy-to-read numerals on its digital face. It is easy to set, with relatively large hour and minute buttons that can be pressed with sore, numb, or stupid fingers. It has a piercing alarm, which escalates to a more frantic tone if not turned off quickly.

It wakes me promptly at 0215. I realize I've fallen asleep and rush up the companionway and look around. There are lights, but well to the south: a ship heading east into the Channel, well inside the traffic separation zones. (Such zones, in the English Channel and in other waters worldwide where there is heavy convergence of shipping into relatively tight areas, are, unlike shipping lanes out at sea, rigidly adhered to; at the other end of the Channel, where barely ten miles of water separates Dover from Calais, traffic is controlled as it is in airports, by controllers glued to radar screens.) There's nothing else in the waters around me now—that I can see. Bishop Rock light at the southern end of the Scilly Islands, flashing twice every fifteen seconds, is visible, ahead and just to starboard, exactly where it should be. I go below, set the alarm, and am soon asleep again.

I continue sleeping through the night, fifteen minutes at a time, waking, looking out, and going easily back to sleep within two or three minutes. By 0800 I no longer feel sleepy. I make toast and coffee and have breakfast sitting in the cockpit looking at the Scilly Islands, small, round, green, and inviting, six miles to the north.

I have traveled to the Scillies by yacht once before. In my early twenties I concocted, with a friend, Bill, a plan to buy a sailboat, cruise down to Morocco, fill it with hashish, and sail it across the Atlantic to the States. Bill had done some sailing; he even thought he knew how to navigate. I had crossed the Atlantic at the age of nine aboard the Cunard liner *Caronia* and been aboard a few cross-Channel ferries. We convinced a friend of my mother's to finance us in return for a third share; bought a wooden schooner, the *Mary Nell*, in Swansea, Wales; filled it with some groceries; and took off.

We sailed out into the Bristol Channel in March. That was when I heard my first BBC shipping forecast: it wasn't good. We were overtaken by a "vigorous low." The sea became alpine, the air turned arctic. We were blown off our intended course. Bill discovered that out of sight of land he had difficulty determining our position. I developed what a yachtsman's medical book we had aboard described as "the third and final stage of seasickness, preceding death." After losing everything in my stomach, I still could not stop retching. I couldn't eat or drink. I couldn't move. All I could do, and did often, was yell and scream at Bill to get us ashore. After three days and three nights of this, Bill put out a radio call asking for help. An hour later, out of the gray, foam-streaked mists, hove a Russian factory trawler, top-heavy with radio antennae. Unasked, without preamble, the Russians shot rocket-propelled grapnels on the end of long lines into the *Mary Nell*'s rigging, where the grapnels successfully entangled themselves. The Russians winched us into the side of their ship, against which the seas threw our boat, smashing both masts, which fell in a tangle of wood and rigging wire onto the deck, as if cannon-shot.

The noise of this, and the sight of the black wall through the porthole above my bunk, brought me out of my vomit-flecked coma with a surge of relief. I thought Bill had got us ashore, alongside some building, and I came up through the hatch ready to leap onto it. What I saw, however, was a group of Russian seamen looking down at us from what seemed a great height. Bill was screaming at them—he was calling them "Russian bastards"—and cutting away the rocket lines with a knife. Every three or four seconds the swell raised us fifteen feet and smashed our hull and the stumps of our masts against the black and rusty side of the trawler. I was confused and terribly disappointed, and I went below again.

Sometime that night we were towed into Hugh Town, on the island of St. Mary's, in the Scillies—I had no idea at the time where that was—by the St. Mary's lifeboat. I was lifted out of our wrecked schooner and taken ashore to the hospital.

During the next few days, Bill and I were a little tense with each other and spent long hours apart. Between cleaning up the boat and filing a report with Lloyd's of being attacked by Russians on the high seas, I wandered over the little island of St. Mary's, which was green and English-looking until you reached its Caribbean white beaches and clear blue water. I gradually became amazed that I had come there, like Gulliver, out of a storm, to a place I'd never heard of, a place so completely unanticipated, a place no one else ever went to (in March, anyway) except people on small boats (and also, apparently, former Prime Minister Harold Wilson, by helicopter, for his holidays). The local Scillonians treated us well, not at all like tourists. They opened themselves up to us, invited us into their homes and lives.

The schooner's cabin, once we had cleaned it up, felt like home in this strange port. It was full of our stuff, our own clothes and books and dinner plates and coffee mugs and pillows. It was a good place to get back to after tramping around the island or talking with the locals at the pub about those bastard Russians.

Despite the ordeal, the seasickness, I began dimly to sense that on a sailboat you could slip through some membrane at the limit of ordinary travel into a world you could never know by any other means. It was the *way* you got there, the difficult, even scary passage, so profoundly unlike a brief hop on a passenger aircraft, or even a ferryboat, that made the destination stand out in vivid relief, as if seen through the clarifier of ion-charged air after a storm. And it was the way the local people saw you, as someone who had traveled there by your own effort, perhaps at some peril, by a means that arouses a sense of romance and adventure in anyone but the dullest stick-in-the-mud. They appreciated it and they took you in.

"We from the little ships, making our brief visits, see and hear things which are not always vouchsafed to the ordinary traveller," wrote the author of a book I found in a local store in St. Mary's. I had not yet heard of Eric Hiscock. The book, *Around the World in Wanderer III*, was his account of the first circumnavigation he and

Susan made in their wooden thirty-foot sailboat, in 1952–5. People like to point to books and say, *This one changed my life.* This was one that changed mine. It wasn't Eric's descriptions of palm-fringed lagoons that excited me, but the vision of refuge that life aboard their little boat offered:

> For four days we lay weather-bound there [at anchor off a nameless islet inside Australia's Great Barrier Reef]. We took the opportunity to catch up with our letter-writing, but the tapping of the typewriter did not drown the doleful whine of the gale. To port of us lay the low green line of the island and to starboard, three miles away and only occasionally visible through the mist, stood the barren, uninhabited coast.

Wherever this was, I discovered it was someplace I wanted to be, inside the same small wooden boat, with gimballed kerosene lamps throwing a cozy glow onto the woodwork, waiting for the weather to subside before sailing off toward somewhere else. For years I remembered this passage from this book. I read other books, and learned that going to sea in a small yacht needn't be the uncontrollable nightmare Bill and I had experienced. I read that Eric and Susan got seasick too, but that in time it afflicted them less. Years later J. and I bought *Toad*, a boat very similar to *Wanderer III*. I became less and less afflicted by seasickness. J. read Hiscock and got the same bug that had gotten me, and we set about slowly and painfully trying to get to that place we both thought we wanted to go.

In another book, *Wandering Under Sail*, Hiscock had written: "Each time I go to Scilly I wonder more and more why I ever bother to go anywhere else, and if ever I own a yacht large enough to carry a good sailing dinghy on deck, I do not think I shall." He wrote this in 1936 or 1937, and though he later had a succession of larger yachts, he never went back to the Scillies. I'm not pulling in there now either, remembering my catastrophic awakening as a sailor and knowing what a wonderful place it is, for the same reason: Eric was looking farther afield and was impatient to be gone.*

By noon, the Scilly Islands have disappeared astern. We move on slowly, the wind light and easterly, behind us.

At 1400, I am below reading when a screaming roar louder than anything I've ever heard brings me up on deck faster than the speed of thought. A jet streaks past overhead at what seems like mast height. I think I can actually feel air rushing into the hole created by its passage, but it may also be the combination stroke/heart attack I'm experiencing. The jet suddenly rotates 90 degrees onto the edge of a wing and banks away until it is invisible. When I can think, a minute or so later, I realize my first thought was that I was about to be run down.

Later, a container ship, *American Legend*, overtakes us. I call it on the radio, saying that I am the small yacht about three or four miles off its starboard side, and ask what sort of a radar picture I make. Bob Damrell is the officer on watch who replies. He says *Toad* makes a reasonable but not great radar picture at 3.8 miles. He asks my destination. When I say Camden, Maine, Bob tells me he's from Boothbay. We talk about sailboats for a few minutes. He has delivered yachts to the Virgin Islands and has some land on St. John. I tell

---

*What happened with the dope deal? Our investor, in too deep to abandon ship, paid to have it repaired, and Bill and I went on to Morocco, where we navigated by pulling in at ports and shouting, *"Où sommes-nous?"* We bought the hash and stashed it aboard, inside the emptied water tanks. But we were no longer enjoying each other's company and we both thought one of us might push the other overboard in mid-Atlantic. I got off. Bill and two other crewmembers sailed across the Atlantic, taking longer than Columbus, and with more uncertainty of position. At the end of a lengthy cruise they reached Florida, the dope was sold, and after the investor recouped his long-ballooning investment, he and Bill split $4,000 profit.

him I bought *Toad* in St. Thomas seven years ago and spent most of my three years in the Virgins anchored off St. John. We talk about who we know there, and find we have mutual friends. Bob says he'll be around Boothbay in September, and I tell him to keep an eye out for *Toad*. He wishes me luck. I take it as a good omen.

June 18

This morning, as I loll in the cockpit with a cup of coffee like a vacationer, I see a pod of pilot whales two hundred yards off the port side. Small dark whales, but at least twice the size of most dolphins. They're following the same course I am and overtake me at a slow, steady speed. They breach regularly to breathe, which they do with a gentle exhalation and inhalation I cannot hear across this short distance.

At 0830 I notice fishing boats scattered in a rough line across the horizon ahead. An hour later, nearing that line, sailing slowly between two rustbucket trawlers, the regular patterns across the water grow subtly disturbed. It isn't fish—my first thought, with the whales and boats about—it's some movement of the water within the water around it. I walk to the bow and look at the water as we move slowly across it. The sea here is still virtually flat, but snaking across the surface is a line of pattern disruption looking something like a tide rip. It's not nearly as pronounced as the small waves that are passing unnoticeably beneath us, but as *Toad* moves across this irregular pattern, the rhythm of its progress—something my body has by now grown used to—alters slightly. We don't slow down, but I feel a change.

I go below and look at the soundings on the chart beneath our position. We are crossing over the edge of the continental shelf. We're soaring, slowly, over an undersea cliff edge. Two hundred meters below *Toad*, the bottom has begun an abrupt plunge into abyssal depths. The cold bottom water will be sliding over the edge and falling too, like a slow-motion waterfall. In the 150 or so miles I've traveled since leaving Falmouth, the continental shelf has dropped all of 100 meters. In the next 15 miles it will fall more than 2,000 meters. This afternoon, if we continue our gentle three-to four-knot poke to the southwest, *Toad* will be sailing over the ocean floor in water over 4,000 meters—13,000 feet—deep.

Normally I don't think about what lies beneath a boat when I'm at sea. I'm concerned with the surface of the ocean, the sea state, and the weather. If I think about the subsurface waters around me, I think of the immediate shallows and of the things I may see or encounter: sharks, whales, dolphins, edible fish, floating obstructions. The greater depth, extending down to the blackness of the ocean floor many vertical miles below *Toad*, is too abstract. Bobbing along on top of the ocean, you can't see more than a few fathoms down into the murk around you, even if you bother to look. More likely, you're fiddling with your wind vane, trying to remember to put on sunblock, looking out for ships, navigating, reading about the Maine coast or the *Beagle*'s passage through Tierra del Fuego. Sailing across the ocean surface, I think no more about the boundless deep than I ponder outer space stretching away directly overhead when I get into the car and drive to the movies. Then I'm only vaguely aware of blue or cloudy sky and I'm looking for a parking space. If I were sailing over a transparent ocean, looking down at the plains and ridges and canyons below (the view would be much like that from a jet flying over the American Southwest) I might give it more thought. I might be petrified.

But I do have *The Times Atlas and Encyclopaedia of the Sea* aboard, and now, as we sail off the continental shelf, I open it up. I find a color plate of the continental slope falling away into the bathyal zone, on its way to the abyssal zone. I look at the pictures of the ocean floors and the jagged sea ridge that rises up and has the Azores—where I'm headed—like a snowcap at its top. The cross-section of the ocean water goes from palest milk at the top to deepest indigo at the bottom. A bit of artistic license there, because at the bottom of the ocean it's pitch-black.

I'm curious about the fish here. I want to find out why these fishing boats are stationed very precisely here at the edge of the continental shelf. The atlas doesn't answer this simply, but I deduce from several sections that this edge of the shelf is a convergent region where fish and organisms from the epipelagic zone (surface to about 200 meters down) mingle with fish and organisms migrating upward for food from the mesopelagic zone (200 meters down to 1,000 meters). The edge of the shelf is an interconvergent smorgasbord where everyone comes to eat everyone else. The trawlers and the whales have come to this same place for the same reason.

I like having this book aboard. It turns the awful and inscrutable sea all around you into a delicate and beautifully intricate organism. It helps you see, if you are inclined to see such a thing, divine creation.

Such an understanding of the sea removes the nonsensical fancy that it can contain malevolence. In the worst of weathers, I've never felt the remotest ill will from the sea, or the least recognition. The ocean, like water in a glass, is absolutely impersonal. It makes no distinction between you and your little dreamboat, filled with your photo albums and all your hopes, and the windblown larva of a mayfly, or a barnacle, or a Styrofoam coffee cup. You're just there. The sea is doing its thing. You deal with it as well as you can, with your weather forecasts, your alarm clock, your sextant and chronometer and the rest of your bag of tricks.

Since losing sight of land when the Scillies fell below the horizon behind us, I have navigated by dead reckoning. I've estimated our position by a combination of recorded course, speed, and time elapsed. This agrees with all the activity here at the edge of the continental shelf, and for the moment I know roughly where we are. But it's time to begin celestial navigation, as I will see no more land and have no other checks of our position until I sight the Azores.

Using the sun, the stars, a sextant, a nautical almanac, sight reduction tables (Publication No. 249 for Air Navigation, published by the U.S. Defense Mapping Agency), and a quartz watch, I can pinpoint my position on the face of any ocean. This seems as wonderful to me as it must have to Captain James Cook (probably more, because I understand the problem less than he), who would probably have given his mother to the Sandwich Islanders who killed him in return for my $19 Casio quartz watch. Until the advent of an accurate timepiece, navigators were unable to determine longitude and were at best inspired guessers, often lost. Disasters at sea directly attributable to errors in navigation led the British government in 1714 to offer £20,000—a fortune large enough to enjoy and pass on to heirs—to anyone who could produce a "generally practicable and useful method" of fixing longitudes at sea. This required the production of a "watch-machine" that would tell time at a uniform rate under conditions of cold and heat, aboard a ship tossed about by storm and wave, so that once set at a point of departure it would continue to show the correct time for that place. The difference between the time at that place and any other place would allow a deduction of longitude. This production of a chronometer was the lifework of a carpenter named John Harrison, a mechanical genius so inarticulate and self-deprecating that the government gave him only half the award money in 1765 because he couldn't explain the workings of his clocks satisfactorily or promote them with bravura. And he only got this much on condition that he hand over the four models he had built, which showed the evolution of his methods. The first clock was the size of a Wurlitzer jukebox, and with its exotic spheres, whirligigs, and multiple dials looked more a time-traveling machine. The last and smallest, an outsize pocket watch as large as an Indian River grapefruit, was duplicated by a craftsman named Larcum Kendall and the method became known and replicable. Harrison got the rest of his money in 1773, after the king took an interest in the matter. Harrison's and Kendall's clocks, and their descendants, are displayed in the British National Maritime Museum in Greenwich, England. I've often gone to see them and am always moved by the difficulties early navigators faced, and overcame, enabling me, a poor mathematician, to poke my way across the oceans with such accuracy.

What I don't know about celestial navigation comprises the main text of most primers on the subject. I learned the essentials from an article in a yachting magazine, which I read hundreds of miles offshore, sitting in *Toad*'s cockpit wondering anxiously where I was. Such a situation has much to recommend it over learning at home or in a classroom. The article's author, Stafford Campbell, suggested that since you didn't need to understand the theory of the internal combustion engine to drive a car, he would describe the basic steps of the practice and worry about the theory later. That was exactly what I wanted to read. I later augmented this article with a small book called *Celestial Navigation for Yachtsmen* by Mary Blewitt, which offered a simple pre-Copernican look at this seaman's science (in this book, the heavenly bodies still revolve around the earth). This got me shooting sun and star sights in very little time, and successfully sailing across unmarked stretches of sea, and once I was able to do that, I forgot all about theory. I navigate by rote, looking up numbers in the almanac and sight reduction tables, adding and subtracting them as necessary. This part of it is far simpler than working out the sticker price of a new car. The real skill in celestial navigation has to do with the accuracy with which you can use a sextant on the deck of a small boat tossing about on the sea.

The sextant is a beautifully designed, essentially simple and old-fashioned device—virtually unchanged since Cook's time— enabling the user to see the sun, moon, or a star through a monocular and filtered shades and pull the image down onto the horizon by means of a hinged mirror, and then measure the angle between the user, the horizon, and the celestial body. Taking a sight on a sunny day in smooth conditions is very different from trying it in murky weather in rough seas. Accuracy in such conditions, and the ability to take a quick "snapshot" of the sun when it appears momentarily through the clouds, as the boat simultaneously rises high enough on a swell to glimpse the true horizon, requires practice and confidence. It has been said that a navigator's second thousand sights will show noticeable improvement over the first thousand.

A bit of theory can, of course, help you out. It can teach you tricks and save you time. In the Virgin Islands I met Ed Boden, who had sailed around the world in an engineless wooden boat a few feet smaller than *Toad*. Before circumnavigating, Ed had been a rocket engineer at Jet Propulsion Laboratories in California. He had been on the team that sent the Mercury rockets into space, paving the way for the Apollo program and the moon landings. Ed had been looking at the heavens long before he became a navigator and he knew the theoretical side of it pretty well. He showed me how, with a bit of extrapolation from the nautical almanac, to estimate to within a minute or so when the sun will reach its zenith in the sky at local noon. This allows you to preset the sextant and go out on deck and take your sight in a few minutes, rather than spending twenty minutes or more squinting skyward through the eyepiece, observing the sun's rise to the point where it stops and begins to descend, and getting a crick in your face that makes you look like Charles Laughton's Quasimodo for half an hour afterward. Ed also knew more dirty limericks than any man alive. Every time I saw him—a grinning, limerick-spewing savant—he told me at least four. But this is the only one I remember:

> *There was a young man from Valparaiso*
> *Who said, "About sex there's one thing I do know.*
> *Young boys are fine, fat women divine,*
> *But the Llama, ah! Numero uno."*

I believe my celestially derived positions are usually accurate to within two to three miles. If the weather is rough and the results more uncertain, greater allowance is given. This is accurate enough for a slow-moving boat.

The X I mark on my chart today at local noon is at latitude 49°19' north, longitude 8°40' west; about 150 miles from Falmouth, and just over 1,100 to Fayal in the Azores.

June 19

0045. The alarm goes off and I'm on deck looking around without waking all the way up. This is my state between bouts of sleep: a kind of functional somnambulism during which I am keyed to wake all the way up and take action if necessary. Right now, still foggy with sleep, I nevertheless see, standing out clearly against the moonlit water, the sharp point of a cotter pin on a turnbuckle at the base of the shrouds along the edge of the deck: it's sticking out and might catch and fray the genoa sheet, which runs close to the turnbuckle. It's not catching now, but it could happen. I haven't noticed this possibility until this sleepy moment in the middle of the night. I get out pliers and some electrical tape and go around the boat flattening and taping all the cotter pins, something I meant to do before leaving Falmouth. Never mind, I'll do it now. At the same time, I check the tension in the rigging, removing pins, tightening the turnbuckles, putting the pins back in, and taping over them. I look around the horizon again and go below, set the alarm, and fall fast asleep. I'm not sure I've even been awake.

I give more thought to the dreams my alarm pulls me out of every twenty or thirty minutes. I seem to dream all night in vivid color. I'm pulled out of them, I go up and look around, pull sheets or cotter pins, go immediately back to sleep, and slip into a new, brilliant dream.

I've been dreaming of my father, who died a year ago, a day before his sixty-first birthday. He got prostate cancer and paid too little attention to it. It metastasized and spread to his spine and grew around it with a strong squeezing grip, removing feeling below his waist and the use of his legs. He had always been an unusually healthy man. His idea of a snack was a piece of celery. He was a great swimmer, with the tall, lean body of an athlete. Things got sticky between us when he and my mother broke up. I found myself championing what I thought was her fair position when they split up their property, and he and I grew estranged for a while. Later we pretended to forget all about it, but I felt an unease between us until he died. I tried to speak about it though he said it didn't matter, yet I knew it did, and he died with this unresolved between us. I've waited for grief, but it hasn't come yet. It's biding its time. My last impression of him was of a man grown suddenly old, emaciated, feeble, and paralyzed. In my dreams he's whole and laughing and younger, his eternal best self, his long arms spread open for me.

At noon today we are at 47°33' north, 13°36' west. Give or take a few minutes. Marking my X at these coordinates on the chart, a chart marked with the positions from previous trips, I see that this is about five miles from another X, *Toad*'s noon position on September 19, nine months ago, when J. and I brought the boat up from Ibiza in the Mediterranean to Falmouth. We left Spain late and got clobbered by two fast-moving equinoctial gales as we neared England.

I have with me the logbook from that trip and I open it now to see what was going on with us that day:

0100: Ship just passed "9 cables" astern—called him up to ask if he'd seen us on radar; he had and we'd made a good picture. He's bound for U.S. and Mexico—it will take him 9 days!

0300: Becalmed. Thunder and lightning out.

1445: Under way at last with light NW'ly. BBC reports low to the S of us, and another NW of us, and gale warnings, but we're headed in the right direction. Large NW'ly swell, gray sky.

On the left-hand page of the logbook, I have written down the salient details of the BBC forecast:

Sole: variable, force 3, becoming SW'ly 5–7, veering NW'ly, gale fore 8.

I flip the page to September 20. We sailed fast all day, and the gale caught up with us around seven that evening.

September 20: 2030: Wind up considerably, seas quite large; reefed main till it's about the size of staysail. Barometer dropping.

At 2200, the log records the wind at force 8 to 9 (thirty-four to forty-seven knots). Worrying about our old sails blowing out, we dropped them all and *Toad* lay "ahull"—that is, no sail up, beam on to the waves, drifting downward, creating a noticeable slick on the water's surface to windward, which, in theory, is supposed to interrupt the advancing waves, causing them to break or topple before they reach and smash into the boat. This seemed to be working, and J. noted that we were lying "comfortably."*

*I would not today lie ahull, even with old and tired sails. I no longer believe this is a seamanlike tactic for heavy weather. Instead, I would "heave-to," that is, put up some scrap of reefed mainsail, however small, and possibly also the smallest headsail "backed," or sheeted to windward, and tie the tiller "down" to leeward. Never mind that this sounds rather technical; it's simple to do. So arranged, a boat will point its bow slightly up to windward and bob quite comfortably, making perhaps a knot of drift at right angles to the wind. In this position the boat does not present its whole broadside, its most vulnerable aspect, to the oncoming waves, as it will do when ahull, but points obliquely into them with its bow, parting them and riding over them. *Heavy Weather Sailing* by the late English author and sailor Adlard Coles, the definitive book on heavy-weather tactics at sea, is filled with anecdotes of disasters resulting from boats lying ahull, but nowhere contains any record of a yacht incurring damage while hove-to. If my small scrap of sail ripped while hove-to, I guess I'd have to lower it, sew it up as best I could, and raise it again. I'd do that standing on deck, tied to something, rather than lie ahull.

The next day, September 21, the BBC reported that this blow was the remainder of tropical storm Debbie.

Two days later, September 23, 88 miles from Falmouth, the forecast was for southwesterly winds force 7 to 8 and "severe gale 9." That night the air was cold and the sky was unusually clear. I took compass bearings on Bishop's Rock light, south of the Scillies, and on Lizard light: 45 miles from the Lizard, well beyond the 29-mile range of its light, its loom was clearly visible above the horizon, pinpointing its position. The wind rose all night, to gale force and beyond, and shifted not to the northwest as expected, but stopped in the south, on our beam, threatening to make it impossible for us to hold our course to pass south of the Lizard and to blow us instead up into the Irish Sea. Reading the log now, I remember that night well, sitting in the cockpit steering, pinching up to windward—to the south—as much as possible, my streaming eyes fixed on Lizard light flashing ahead, willing it to stay on the bow and even begin slipping to port, which, finally, in the wee hours, it did. We blew into Falmouth in wild rain squalls just after noon the next day. We sailed past the town up the Flushing River and anchored in flat water surrounded by green hills.

That was J.'s and my last trip together. I remember it all clearly as I read the logbook and sail on alone in the gentlest of conditions toward the Azores. As always, we derived great comfort from each other in bad weather, but the rest of the passage had been flat. We

---

I've reached this conclusion mostly from further reading. I've never experienced "survival" weather conditions at sea. The finest essay I've read on storm tactics for small boat sailors is the appendix of Miles Smeeton's *Because the Horn Is There*. Smeeton and his wife, Beryl, were twice dismasted aboard their yacht *Tzu Hang* west of Cape Horn, the first time "pitchpoled" (the boat somersaulted) while running downwind before a great gale, the second time rolled over while lying ahull. Years later they successfully rounded the Horn in *Tzu Hang*. Smeeton wrote that he would never again lie ahull, and his thoughts on tactics, confirmed by his own wide reading of other sailing narratives, are to be respected.

no longer shared the trip as we used to, talking endlessly as we prepared meals and navigated and tucked each other in and kissed each other at the beginning and end of every watch, planning future voyages, and the "next boat," the dream boat we would build together and sail around the world. That was something we had talked about for years, and had stopped talking about. We were often silent, keeping our thoughts to ourselves, moving about the tiny boat on our own errands, trying not to make trouble. Trying not to have the sort of fight we'd had as we sailed past Cape St. Vincent and into the lee of the European continent at the end of our transatlantic passage the year before, when we should have been hugging each other and toasting our achievement, but instead had been screaming how fucking sick to death we were of each other. That had been a milestone. We stayed together another year, living in London, wondering what had happened and what we were doing. Then we brought *Toad* up to Falmouth, went back to London, and one day split up.

I have all our old logbooks aboard. I start going through some of the others, reading back to find when it had been good. But it all looks good in the logbooks: references to wind and sea, food we like, ships, visiting dolphins, two birds flying together, a fish caught, a turtle overtaking us, the cats' insatiable appetite for flying fish, a birthday breakfast for J. as we approach Bermuda slowly but in perfect weather. We didn't record the fights or the ugly things we said to each other.

The old logbooks are full of references to our attempts to get the wind vane to steer the boat. The vane gear is an inelegantly homemade affair of plywood, stainless steel tube and strapping, nuts, bolts, and string. It came with the boat and was bent up and torn off when another boat collided with us in St. Thomas. I then rebuilt it. It worked adequately about half the time. But when winds were light or from astern (when the apparent wind is reduced by the speed of the boat moving away from it), the gear would not overpower the boat's natural and proper tendency to head up to windward unless we deeply reefed the mainsail, reducing our speed—not what you want to do in light and favorable winds. At other times, in conditions that had suited the gear one day, it would turn ornery and refuse to steer the next, and then J. and I would have to steer.

As I skipped the theory part of celestial navigation, I have similarly bothered little over the years with the aero- and hydrodynamic business of how a sailboat works. I have read that the wind doesn't, in fact, push a sailboat, but creates a vacuum on the leeward, or backside, of a sail, and the boat is apparently sucked along by this vacuum. Sitting on a boat that's being blown about by the wind—feeling myself blown about too, feeling the wind push me rather than any vacuum hauling at me—I find I don't respond well to the idea that what I appear to be seeing and feeling isn't really happening. I can grasp the theory, I've seen all the diagrams, and I've heard people expounding on the principle. It doesn't appeal to me. And I've found I can do perfectly well without it. I prefer to base my actions on my own crude, empirical experience. I've spent seven years sailing the engineless *Toad* across about 15,000 miles of water by fiddling with its sails, feeling the wind on my face or the back of my neck, looking at the water around us, and watching it flow along *Toad*'s hull and tumble into the wake astern, and this has taught me what I know. (I've also sailed about 10,000 miles in other, newer boats, delivering them between ports for paying customers, and this has provided a welcome chance to observe the behavior of different types of boats in all sorts of weather. This experience I brought to my efforts at handling *Toad*.)

Sailing thus, while also trying to get the vane gear to work, I've learned what I know about sail trim and the balance of a sailboat, and over time this has meant more hours when I could get the whole contraption, boat and wind vane gear together, to hold a steady course.

But I wanted more from the vane: I wanted a wind vane that

steered all courses in all conditions. You can buy them in yacht chandlers, and they have always cost more than I could afford. Their smug owners rave about them in ports and anchorages where cruisers get together. So I bought John Letcher's book this winter and made some alterations to the gear while *Toad* was hauled out in Mylor and I was being harangued by Wilfred. The difference is tremendous. The gear suddenly has a sensitivity and power I had not even hoped for. Undistractable, sensitive to every puff and zephyr, the plywood vane constantly turns itself slightly to one side or the other as the boat yaws, like someone hard of hearing angling his head from one side to another. It now steers better than I can. I removed the tiller from the rudderhead as *Toad* sailed past Martin on Pendennis Point and have not touched it since. All this time the wind has been light and from behind us and the gear has steered the boat.

This has affected my life aboard *Toad* more than anything else. I now have all the time I want to read, prepare my meals, navigate, sit on the bowsprit when the dolphins come and watch them, in pairs, crisscrossing in the water immediately below me, or sit and do nothing. I watch the sea and sky for longer periods now without glancing at the compass. I see their constant change. See a cloud for a second and it's a static photograph. Lie on the foredeck and watch it for fifteen minutes and it evolves into a wraithlike organism. Trade wind clouds are marvelous to look at: small, dense, and regular as sheep, an infinite flock low overhead ambling toward the western horizon. All day, by degrees more perceptible the longer you watch, the light and the sea change. From looking through the sextant you know already the incredible speed at which the day's seemingly steady features are evolving: the sun shoots up to its zenith so fast that to hold it down on the horizon you must constantly adjust the instrument.

Cloud, light, and darkness create spatial sensations of "places" I sail through to new places, as if moving from room to room. At night this impression intensifies, all scale is lost, the rooms grow as tall as the clouds that form their walls and ceilings, and I am the tiniest toddler on a wet rocking horse moving through a giant moonshot house of elastic shapes and perspectives. Makes me think of acid hallucinations in the sixties. I wonder now if I'm hallucinating or seeing what's really there.

June 20

This morning, sorting through bags of old clothes up forward, I come across the yellow sail bag.

It has been here, stashed in its corner of the forepeak, for years. Yellow dacron, cinched at the top with a drawstring, a blue base, and the word MAINSAIL stenciled onto it. Not a bag for one of *Toad*'s sails, it belonged to a charter company in St. Thomas and was being thrown out when J. and I, wharf-rat scroungers, spotted it and took it home. We've used it as a laundry bag, a carryall duffel for our clothes and gear when we took off delivering other people's boats, but it has found its most lasting use as a place to store old papers, letters, junk we no longer use but perhaps don't want to throw out. It's our cardboard box in the basement.

I drag it aft into the saloon. I'm sure most of its contents—biodegradable paper—can now be thrown overboard.

J. has not been back aboard *Toad* since we split up. We were in London then. She had her foul-weather gear and boots and some clothes with her and she went straight to Nice to stay with her mother. She hasn't taken anything off *Toad*, but we don't own much that isn't screwed into the boat.

I open the bag.

On the top, sitting on all the papers and the useless junk, are J.'s diaries covering the first five years of our marriage. Hardcover lined notebooks, the year stamped on the cover, a page per day. The pages are swollen with damp, but all the books are in readable condition. When we were together, her diaries were always lying around, on a shelf in the saloon, and she wrote in them almost every day. But I've never opened them. Now I open the first book at April 23 and spores of memory rise off the page: the Millstream Hotel in Bosham, West Sussex . . . J.'s bridal bouquet of freesias and lilies of the valley . . .

I remember, of course. In the middle of the ceremony at the pretty Norman church, J. and I succumbed momentarily to a barely audible, nervous giggle, and the vicar stopped dead in the middle of reciting for me to repeat "and thereto I plight thee my troth" and stared at us with the expression of an irate schoolteacher. He stared at each of us in turn, from one to the other, until I thought he was going to close his Bible and tell us to leave. Twice I tried to jump-start him back into the ceremony by saying, "And thereto I plight thee my troth." Finally, after an embarrassing pause, he went on. It was a prophetic interruption.

I flip the page and find a brown stem, brown leaves, and a crumbling brown flower pressed between April 25 and 26.

I turn pages. We left England the day after our wedding and drove to Porto Ercole in Italy, where we picked up my parents' forty-four-foot ketch. They had bought the boat as their marriage was foundering, thinking they would sail away and things would get better. They named it *Viva III*, meaning that it was to be their third life together. The first had been in the States, when they had met in Greenwich Village after the war, had kids, and moved out to suburban Connecticut. The second life had been in England, where they had moved with three young kids in 1959. Their *Viva III* lasted a year. At the time of our wedding, my father was living with his second wife in Orvieto, Italy; the boat was for sale, and J. and I were going to try to run it as a charter boat in the south of France until it sold. I had done a little crewing aboard other sailboats after the infamous dope run and had sailed often aboard my parents' boat with them during the year they spent in the Mediterranean before breaking up, and I knew enough by then to look after the boat.

Our honeymoon cruise from Porto Ercole to St. Jean Cap Ferrat was J.'s first sail. She writes of her worries that she would be able to cope.

May 7 begins with an entry saying that she has had nightmares about me. I don't know what this means. I flip on.

On May 11 we kissed in the cockpit and played with ropes and knots as we approached St. Jean Cap Ferrat on the French coast after a lumpy day-and-night sail from Corsica. Then the engine died. Our VHF call to the Capitainerie at St. Jean was answered by Sven Bergstrom, who came out in a motorboat with his wife, Ingrid, and son, Leif, who managed to start the engine.

This was a fateful meeting. My parents had met Sven, his second wife, Ingrid, and his son, Leif, by his first wife, when they had passed through St. Jean during their brief *Viva III*. The Bergstroms lived aboard their fifty-foot ketch *Vagabond* in St. Jean, and they remembered *Viva III*. Leif, then in his early twenties, was shy and very quiet, and turned red whenever J. spoke to him. We saw the Bergstroms often during that summer and several times in the years that followed. When J. went to stay with her mother in Nice after we split up, she looked up the Bergstroms again. Leif, now a proficient engineer and yacht captain, was delivering a large motor yacht to the Caribbean, and J. went with him. They're still together.

I read on in her diary, riveted by the ordinary details of our days that rise off the diary pages like forgotten aromas. On May 12 the Volvo man promised to come look at the engine the next day. That evening we ate *moules* and pizza at Joe's Pizzeria in St. Jean and saw the actor Oliver Reed, drunk, at the next table. . . . Drinks with the Bergstroms aboard *Vagabond*. . . . Local yacht broker Gérard Spriet came to appraise the boat, and felt it was worth $75,000, rather than the $100,000 my parents wanted. . . . Martin wrote to tell us of a possible charter. . . . Sunday lunch with my friends Peter and Jennie, who lived in St. Jeannet. . . . A drive (we had brought my old Morris up from Italy after the boat trip) to Sospel in the forested hills above Menton where we had a picnic. . . .

Like waking from a dream, I look up from J.'s diary and see blue sky and clouds arcing through the porthole across the saloon, hear the waves running past the outside of the hull. Normally I have a good memory, but this virtual time capsule takes me back into vivid and complete scenes where I can look around and see beyond what she has recorded, at what I've long forgotten. I remember only now the church in Sospel: we went inside after the picnic and saw photographs of dead parishioners on pale blue plaster walls, formal black and white portraits of dead woodsmen and farmers and their wives and children taken too soon.

What I've forgotten, and remember more slowly, is that J. and I fought with each other from the very beginning. And I've forgotten, or little knew, the degree of her uncertainty about us and her strong ambivalence toward me. She writes, over and over, that she is unhappy . . . depressed . . . we have another fight . . . make up . . . fight again . . . we're both unhappy . . . distant . . . another fight . . . depressed . . .

Page after page of this—weeks of it—and it takes me by surprise. Maybe it was to be expected. Although we'd known each other for years, we had only lived together a short while before marrying. I had pulled her away from José. We were adjusting to each other. But she was also excited by living on the boat, and the diary shows this too.

Reading of good days or bad, it's all painful stuff right now. I close the diary and put it away with the other four in a saloon cupboard.

I go up on deck and am back into my own solitary voyage.

Five days out. The barometer is beginning to drop as we move away from the high still centered west of Ireland. The BBC reports a low over Portugal. The counterclockwise flow of wind at the top of the low, southeast of us, is combining with the clockwise flow at the bottom of the high, to the northeast. Both blow at us from the same direction, still from astern, but now the wind picks up. By dusk it's blowing about force 5, the strongest wind we've felt so far. I reef the main and now go out onto the end of the bowsprit to remove the large lightweight genoa and put on the older, smaller, heavier one. As I'm doing this, the genoa's sailbag blows overboard. I don't stop and go back for it; it would take many minutes to disconnect the vane and get us sailing back on a reciprocal course. And then I know I wouldn't find it. I just sit and watch the bag become smaller and disappear into the growing darkness astern.

It's no leap to imagine it's me in the water being left behind as night comes on. I'm not wearing my harness, though I have one, made of nylon webbing, which would attach me to the boat by a short length of line and a snap shackle. It's stashed below. J. and I wore our harnesses occasionally, mostly during bad weather, and as much as anything because the greatest fear each of us had was that one of us would wake up and find the other gone. I don't worry about that now. I don't have J. saying, "Have you got your harness on?" If I do go overboard the wind vane will ensure that *Toad* will sail on without me.

I don't like harnesses. They can make you move around the boat in short, awkward stops and starts, clipping yourself on and off, undermining your natural balance. After a day or two at sea, the body unconsciously accommodates itself to the movement of a small boat. You find yourself moving fluidly up and down the deck. Interrupting this to clip on and off every few feet, and overreliance on a harness, are, I believe, more likely than anything else to propel you overboard and kill you.

This is my prejudice. It's also a common rationalization among those sailors who choose not to wear harnesses all the time. Others hotly disagree. Many sailors believe you should wear a harness anytime you leave the apparent safety of the cockpit.

Harnesses have unquestionably saved people. And harnesses have failed. Of 235 crew who said they wore harnesses during the 1979 Fastnet Race, between England and Ireland, twenty-six (11 percent!) reported harness failures—either buckles came undone, hooks straightened out, attachment points broke, or safety lines chafed through. Six lives were lost directly as a result of these failures. Ten crewmembers reported that harness lines wrapping around obstructions prevented them from climbing back aboard unassisted.

People have been tossed overboard during vulnerable moments

between clip-on points. Our friend from St. Jean, Ingrid Bergstrom, coming out of *Vagabond*'s companionway, wearing a harness but not yet having reached a clip-on point, was tossed overboard at night in a gale in the Mediterranean, a certain death sentence. Her husband Sven rang a deck bell that summoned Leif to the cockpit. "Ingrid's gone overboard," he said. "Hold this course." Sven went below to the chart table and, despite a mind reeling from shock, calculated what ground would be lost turning around, drift from wind and waves, the boat's reciprocal course and likely speed, and the speed and time elapsed since Ingrid had gone overboard, then mixed all these together and plotted a new course back to that spot. He went back up to the cockpit and *only then* did he and Leif turn the boat around and go back along the course he had decided upon to look for her. They found her and got her aboard. A miracle.

Reliance on safety harnesses—a modern device—has meant a widespread atrophy of that best of all devices to keep you aboard: a fully developed horror of falling overboard. Aboard commercial sailing ships in the past, sailors relied on this above all measures. When men had to turn out at a moment's notice and run along the deck and scramble upward through the rigging, such tying-on would have been impossible, and laughable. Joshua Slocum, the first man to sail singlehanded around the world, did not know how to swim and did not wear a harness. (To be fair, it must be admitted that he disappeared at sea on a subsequent voyage, along with his boat.) A determined refusal to go overboard, and a number of precautions—an overall design—taken to ensure that you stay aboard puts the wearing of a harness in its proper place: an additional measure, rather than a single, fallible device.

I wear my harness mostly during bad weather, particularly if I'm going to leave the cockpit and go forward or out on the bowsprit. Otherwise, more usually, I rely on my own inner gyroscope, on sail-handling tactics designed to avoid my exposure to risk, and on premeditated thought and visualization of how I am going to move about the boat. I rely, far more than on my harness, on the additional lifelines I've strung around the perimeter of the boat. *Toad* has the standard lifelines you see on most yachts, running between stanchions at heights of fifteen and thirty inches above the deck. These can help keep you from rolling off the deck, but if you're standing up and collide forcibly with them they can buckle your legs and flip you into the sea as gracefully as a Flying Wallenda. To avoid this, before I left port I ran a three-eighths-inch nylon line (breaking strength thirty-seven hundred pounds, with great elasticity) from bowsprit tip to stern, fixed at the rigging shrouds, down both sides of the boat at chest level. The effect is something like being in a boxing ring. It will be difficult to get through this cordon at fifteen, thirty, and fifty inches above the deck. This upper line gives me a tremendous sense of security. I automatically run my hand along it as I move around the deck, in calm or wind. I lean against it when taking sextant sights. I believe this is far more effective than any harness, and when I wear my harness I clip its snap shackle to this line and thus continue to move freely up and down the deck.

But most of all I rely on my fear of falling overboard. I have imagined being in the water and watching *Toad* sail away from me. That's enough.

Of course, it can still happen. I know that. But I believe it's one of those things that's more unlikely than being knocked down by a bus. And then it won't matter if I'm wearing clean underwear or not.

I watch the sailbag growing smaller astern, floating as long as I can see it.

I go below and eat spaghetti and listen to a Joni Mitchell concert on the BBC's shortwave World Service.

Day after day the weather remains fair. The barometer rises again. Does this mean the high has shifted to the west and we are back in it? I don't know. We've sailed beyond the range of the BBC's FM shipping forecast; I have to figure it out for myself now. The high's concentric isobars may have wobbled and elongated, like the stuff in those tacky liquid lava lamps you used to see in the seventies, and joined up with the great high usually hovering over the central Atlantic at this time of year. I don't know, but I'm grateful the wind is still blowing out of the east, the northeast, sometimes the north, shifting back and forth and giving me something to do as I change sail arrangements—but still behind us or out on the starboard quarter, and pushing us gently, directly toward the Azores.

Days run into one another, marked by small things. On the evening of June 20 we pass the 500-mile mark from Falmouth.

June 21

0200: I come on deck and look around. No lights. We're alone on the whole visible surface of the sea. I watch *Toad* surging on without any help from me, all sails trimmed and pulling, the wind vane steering an accurate course. Pointing straight at the Azores, 700 miles ahead, the boat seems to know where it's going, and plows on with steady, dogged enthusiasm. It's been doing this for five days now, all by itself. I can't believe at this moment that this is no more than a man-made machine, an assembly of wood, screws, bolts, wire, and cloth, without a sentient notion of what it's up to. *I can see it* feeling the sea, meeting and shouldering its way through every wave with understanding and skill. And it will go on and on doing this, without any fuel, without any help from me, until I make it stop. To me this seems as miraculous as perpetual motion. I sit on the cabin roof as we move through the dark, and watch this for a while.

Later in the night I wake and look out the hatch and find we're sailing in company with another pod of pilot whales. They're puffing along rhythmically about a hundred yards off our starboard side, very slowly overtaking. They're not large, and in the dark it's their slow, purposeful, unplaying cruising speed that distinguishes them most from the ever-exuberant dolphins. I look at the trim of the sails and tweak them to see if we can gain a half a knot or so and give the whales a race. But we're doing our best, it seems, and the whales slowly pull ahead. I go back to sleep.

0800: Wind up. Still abeam (NW). Bombing along and making great progress. Finished last of Falmouth store-bought bread for breakfast. Will have to get baking.

0920: 2 LOPs ["line of position" sextant sights] snatched early as it's becoming cloudy and overcast—might not find the sun later. Log 556. Have been having fun reading my New England Cruising guide looking for first landfall in Maine. Camden looks nice but crowded, and I might have to pay for a mooring—that's out. Burnt Coat Harbor, Swans Is. looks good.

1315: Noon pos: 45°57'N, 18°20'W. 110 miles noon to noon. About 650 miles to Horta—almost halfway.

1900: Reading Henry Beston's Outermost House. Wonderful winter storms on Cape Cod.

Seventh day out, this is also J.'s birthday, our first apart in seven years. If I were ashore today I would . . . I don't know . . . send her a telegram, maybe. Or just accept it. All day I've thought about her other birthdays, where we were and what we did. I am still getting used to the idea of sailing alone without her. She is a great reproachful silence aboard the boat at times. But the practice of sailing without her—the management of the boat on my own, getting enough sleep, being without her or any other soul to talk to, is so far working well. I have fantasized about sailing singlehanded for years, wondered what it would be like, how I'd cope with being so alone, and I'm almost surprised to find that I seem to be enjoying it as much as I thought I would. I am lonely, but not with the crushing loneliness I have felt in large cities that can leave you feeling like some unfortunate biblical type "cast out" from his own kind to wander the earth alone. Like, say, Wilfred in Mylor. This loneliness is often an exquisite state that takes time to recognize and savor, something I'm just beginning to get the hang of and enjoy. Something I know I wouldn't feel with J. or anyone else aboard the boat with me.

I have in fact come to the conclusion that sailing alone seems easier than with J. There is no tension, anxiety, or unhappiness aboard the boat anymore. I don't worry about her, about whether she's fallen overboard, or if she's as afraid as I am. Or if she's happy, which was always my greatest worry. And, looking back, my greatest failure. Alone seems better, for the moment.

Tonight I put aside The Outermost House and take up J.'s innermost scribbles and look back to see what happened on June 21 seven years ago, in the south of France.

It was a Monday. I gave her Cousteau's book about sharks, which always fascinated her. She has recorded the food we ate all day, from the honeyed grapefruit I baked in *Viva*'s oven for her breakfast to the ingredients of the picnic we packed and took to St. Tropez—white wine, baguette, pâté, Camembert, melon—and dinner at a Vietnamese restaurant in Nice's old port: *pho* noodle soup and some fish. She writes that she has pressed a rose from there into this diary . . . so that's the brown thing many pages back that I thought might have come from her wedding bouquet. After dinner we drove on to St. Jean, where we danced (though P. was stiff). A happy day. And she writes: "*merci P . . .*" at the bottom of the page.

Birthday over, I keep turning pages, held by the fascination of seeing another view of scenes I remember, and remembering again what I've forgotten.

Our naive honeymoon plan of turning up in the south of France with my parents' boat and spending the summer raking in charter fees was quickly dashed. We were too late. We presented ourselves to the local charter agents everywhere along the coast between Monaco and Cannes, and were told that most bookings were made well before the season, usually six to twelve months in advance. There was little last-minute business. There were many beautiful yachts. But the agents, most of them, looked at us and found compassion enough to say nice things about our brochure for *Viva III*, which we'd had printed in London, and promised us they would keep us in mind.

We soon ran completely out of money. We'd been given a little by our families at our wedding, but after a month and a half of supporting the boat, buying paint, varnish, fuel, and paying the steep dock fees in lovely St. Jean Cap Ferrat, it was all gone. We'd watched it going with little concern, until the very end, believing that the boat was so beautiful, someone would come down the dock and want to spend a few glorious days aboard it. Also, the boat was seriously for sale, listed at all the yacht agencies on the coast, and people were coming to look at it; it was possible someone would buy it at any moment. But no one chartered, the boat remained unsold, and finally we had to leave the port. We had to find the cheapest place to keep a boat on that stretch of Riviera. That turned out to be the middle of the harbor in Monaco. You could drop your anchor there, tie a stern line to one of the harbor's mooring buoys, for 40 francs a week, or $8.

We still had my car, an old Morris Traveller, the wood rotting along its sides and growing mushrooms. As we drove up and down the coast visiting charter agents, we tried to fend off desperation by picnicking in the Provençal hills, but even that palled as we fretted over every centime.

Oliver Reed finally rescued us from penury on the Riviera. He had bought a sixty-foot Chinese junk, which lay in Beaulieu, next to St. Jean Cap Ferrat. An Englishman named Tony, a very smooth fellow whom we'd met in every bar in St. Jean, managed to get himself appointed captain of "Ollie's" junk, and he hired J. and me to scrape and revarnish its entire teak hull.

Flush with francs, we dined out after our first day's work, on *coquille de fruits de mer, salades, tarte aux framboises, vin de maison* (on almost every day, J. has recorded what we ate). And from Tony we bought two tickets for Nice's upcoming jazz festival, a leaflet for which is pressed between July 7 and 8.

And our fighting—recorded as faithfully as our diet—continued despite good food and music.

I flip pages, passing through weeks. Work, money, wonderful food, fights, and J.'s record of the minutiae of our daily life: a broken public phone in Beaulieu from which we could make free calls, my haircut from an old-fashioned gents barber in Monaco, and rainy days that interrupted our work on Ollie's *Ding Hao*, when we would pack a picnic (wine, pâté, Camembert, baguette) and drive off into the hills.

We finished our work on the *Ding Hao* and began to get a few charters, hand-me-downs from other boaters. A newly married middle-aged French couple for a day. Four tiny Irish jockeys and their strapping wives and girlfriends (who all had the long legs of thoroughbreds) for four days.

Then a friend from St. Jean with engine trouble gave us his week with an English family, and we were thrilled. This meant real money. But after a day of Derek, Mavis, and their heavy-footed children thumping all over *Viva*, J. found she couldn't bear them, couldn't mask the sense of violation she felt having them shouting and crashing around in her home, and she begged out. I replaced her with my brother David, who was vacationing in the Provençal hill town of Bargemon with his girlfriend. J. went to Bargemon and David and I sailed Derek, Mavis, and brood to Corsica. They were fine, in fact, loud and rough, perhaps, the boys needing vigilance with the boat's gear, but they also had an endearing capacity to enjoy themselves without a hint of English restraint, and they always respectfully asked me to tell them the best way to do anything. Halfway to Corsica, Derek turned to me and said, "Peter, I'm going to vomit in a minute. Which side of the boat would be best?" Mavis did all the cooking, blackening *Viva*'s pots and pans without fail. "Caught" was the family's word for burnt, and the cry at mealtimes was always an exasperated, "It's caught *again*, Mummy!" I remember them now fondly. And David and I were the best of shipmates together.

Friday, August 13, my birthday. I see I got a Tintin book, *Le Trésor de Rackham Le Rouge*, and a pair of docksiders. In the evening we set off to a restaurant in Menton to meet our friends Peter and Jennie, and David and his girlfriend. Halfway there J. remembered she left the address behind on the boat. We drove back, rushed aboard, and—surprise! They were all there, with food.

One day's page has only the words *"Douanes boat"* written on it, but I remember it in vivid detail. One evening late in the summer we were lying alongside the dock in Beaulieu, J. reading (or maybe writing in the diary I'm reading) in the cockpit, while I was below. I heard voices in the cockpit, J. talking with someone. I didn't pay attention for a few minutes, until I detected a tone of discomfort in her voice. I came up and found a young, swart Mediterranean thug, bare-chested, wearing jeans, leaning into *Viva*'s cockpit, leering at J. I asked him what he wanted. He asked me if I was the boat's owner. Yes, I said, and asked him again what he wanted. I was affronted by him and his loutish unsubtle machismo and I'm sure this showed. He bristled and told me to prepare for an official customs inspection. He walked away, short, muscular, thick-legged, to a large, high-powered *Douanes* launch that had come in earlier. In five minutes he was back, wearing a uniform hat and shirt over his jeans, accompanied by his middle-aged commandant and three other members of the launch's crew.

They boarded *Viva* and searched it from top to bottom. I asked them what they were looking for and the commandant replied that this was a routine inspection. They found nothing; but the boat's green card—*passeport du navire étranger*—the permit for a foreign vessel in French waters, had expired. Ordinarily this was a simple matter of getting it stamped again with a new date. But the commandant now told us we had incurred a fine of 200 francs, payable immediately in cash. I told them we didn't have that much cash on us (true), that I could either give them traveler's checks now, or cash in the morning. Impossible, they were leaving early in the morning, they needed the money now. I offered to pay the fine at the *Douanes* office in Nice tomorrow. "*Non!*" both the commandant and his macho lieutenant said. We had to pay in cash now, tonight, or the fine would be double. They had become astonishingly angry. They said we must know someone from whom we could get the money.

We were tied at the shadowy end of a long dock, away from most of the boats in the port. We were alone with this crew of *douaniers,* and the menace we felt from them was unmistakable, particularly so from the young lieutenant. He was undoubtedly Corsican, almost Arab in appearance, a type seen everywhere along the southern French coast, and he had a hot, mad look in his face that made reason—the plausible appeal that they simply couldn't expect us to produce such a sum of money now, at night, at a moment's notice—useless. As well as wanting money, their eyes were crawling over J. We were afraid.

Okay, I said. We knew where we could get the money. We had friends in St. Jean. We'd go get the money and come right back. This seemed to placate them momentarily. I picked up our keys—for the car and the boat—locked the boat up, and J. and I stepped ashore. I said again that we would go get the money and come right back. We turned, and the lieutenant grabbed J.'s arm. "She stays here," he said.

I exploded, insane with male rage. I yelled in his face, something about how I didn't like being taken for a cretin, that I wasn't leaving my wife with anyone. I grabbed her and we turned and marched away. For a few long seconds they did nothing; I think they were a little amazed at my outburst, which, being in French, they might have been still trying to decipher. But when they saw us abruptly get into the English car sprouting *champignons* along its wooden sides, they started to run. It was a movie getaway: backing out I almost hit them, making them jump back, then, crunching gears, we took off at a sedate pace while they ran after us. It was touch and go with the Morris's acceleration, but we finally pulled ahead and left them behind, still running after us down the dock.

We were stunned. Thrilled by our getaway, but still frightened, and now worried for the boat, thinking the thwarted *douaniers* would board it and trash it. We didn't know what to do. We drove into St. Jean and found Sven Bergstrom aboard *Vagabond*. We told him our story. He was sympathetic but not very surprised. He told us how corrupt everything was along the *côte,* from the notorious racketeer mayor of Nice, Jacques Mèdecin, down to thugs like our *douaniers* who were a law unto themselves. We decided the best plan was to stay away from the boat tonight, go to the *Douanes* office in

Nice in the morning, and report the incident to them. Meanwhile, Sven too was worried about *Viva*. He put on his Swedish naval hat (whether his own or simply a nautical artifact, I don't know; it was heavy with gold braid and looked about right for an admiral), extending his height from six-foot-three to six-six, and with his large, naturally protruberant eyes and close-cropped beard, he made an imposing sight, a figure of undoubted if unspecific authority. He said he'd drive around to Beaulieu on the pretext of visiting us. When he came back half an hour later, he reported that the *douaniers* had approached him as he had called aboard for us. They told him we had gone off somewhere on an errand. They were very respectful to him. He thanked them and left. He said they did not appear to have gone aboard the boat. We were all pleased that at least they wouldn't have their hoped-for night out on us. At least not that night.

J. and I drove into Nice, had dinner in a small restaurant in the old port, and spent the night in a hotel, clinging to each other for sanctuary. In the morning, we told our story to officials at the *Douanes* office. They seemed bewildered. They left us in a room for almost an hour, and when they returned our *douaniers,* in full uniform, were with them. The Corsican screamed at us, accusing us of running from justice. We asked to see the American consul. The local officials seemed embarrassed. When the shouting subsided, we paid the officials 200 francs, our boat's green card was stamped, and we left.

Later that day, back in Beaulieu, in daylight, we watched the *Douanes* launch depart. As it crossed *Viva*'s bow, the Corsican raised his hand and pointed his finger at me, staring, an unmistakable murderous threat should we ever meet again.

We left Beaulieu a little later, bound up the coast to Monaco. Offshore I looked around nervously, half expecting the *Douanes* launch to be lying in wait for us or to appear suddenly from behind a headland and zoom toward us. There was no sign of it. Perhaps its crew were on to richer game, of which there was plenty about. But for the rest of the summer, in port and offshore, I looked around and watched my back for that *Douanes* launch and its crew and wondered what would happen if I saw them.

This pulled us close together. Us against the world we were fine. It was from the inside that trouble came. I've forgotten how frequently and easily J. would slip into depression. And back then I could only conclude that if she was unhappy it must be my fault. And maybe it was. I'm no day at the beach. But my memories triggered by her impressions are poor witnesses to any truth. What single truth is there between two people?

Enough. J.'s birthday draws to an end. I set the alarm and go to sleep.

June 24

0130: Got up for lookout, then feeling awake turned on radio and heard "Alfie" done as radio play by the BBC [shortwave World Service]. Really good.

My radio, a large black Panasonic short- and longwave receiver, is on more than it is off. Out at sea, beyond the range of shore stations, I keep it tuned mostly to the BBC World Service frequencies, or to the Voice of America. The music, news, and eclectic chitchat about every imaginable subject that pours forth effectively produces another presence aboard the boat, like some old auntie tucked away in a corner always just beyond my peripheral vision; someone who has an incredible range of general knowledge, but at the same time is a bit of an old bore, who prattles inanely on and on, whom I can tune in to or ignore as I like, or even turn off at the flick of a switch. But she's always available. I don't know what I'd do without her, except realize how utterly alone I am. She holds that at bay.

0400: Been tearing along broad-reaching all night, great speed. Just picked up U.S. Coast Guard, Portsmouth, VA, doing their Offshore forecast. Must listen at 0530 for their High Seas forecast.

0535: Heard it. Nothing much—low at 42°N, 51°W—far away.

0730: Cloudy, totally overcast. Might be a rainy day. Porridge for breakfast. Good day to tackle Gibbon.

1355: Listened to Shuttle touchdown in California on Voice of America.

1730: Just sailed out from under all that cloud into clear blue skies. Beautiful.

2330: Beautiful moonlit night. Dolphins playing around. Jibed.

June 25

0230: *Just passed a sailboat, quite close. I was in the middle of jibing and had to stop and put on my lights. Afterward came below and found a BASE-BALL GAME on VOA! Can't make out who's playing yet.*

0315: *White Sox and someone.*

1040: *Another sailboat to the SE, tacking NE against my fair wind, poor bugger. Second sailboat in 8 hours. It's too early in the summer to be seeing transatlantic boats this far east. These boats must be on the return leg of the AZAB [Azores And Back Race] out of England, which started from Falmouth a couple of weeks before I left. Haven't expected to see many of them on the direct rhumb line that I'm following. I would think they'd head farther north where they might hope to find westerly winds around the top of this seemingly stationary high.*

1345: *Noon pos: 41°30'N, 25°47'W; 87 miles noon to noon. About 225 miles to Horta—hopefully in 2 days, on the 27th. We're 180 miles from Graciosa, which I want to glimpse, or see its light if we pass it at night.*

I'm growing excited as we near the Azores, and filled with memories. Two years ago, on our way across the Atlantic, eastbound from Florida to the Mediterranean, J. and I spent the whole month of August anchored in the harbor off Horta, Fayal's main town. It was unenterprising of us not to have cruised around the other islands, but we were having too good a time exploring Fayal and talking and eating and partying with other yachties from the United States, England, Brittany, and Scandinavia. We saw again people and boats we'd met in the Caribbean and on the U.S. East Coast, and from them heard news of many others.

A thousand miles west of its owner, Portugal, easily sailed to from all directions, out of the way of most bad weather, Fayal has long been an important crossroad in the Atlantic, a vital link between the New World and the Old. It was a port of call for

Yankee whaling ships that could off-load barrels of oil and cargos of baleen for shipment on to New England, and find new hands for their crews. Native Azoreans, good boat handlers and whalers from small boats ashore, were prized additions to any whaling ship. So many embarked here, cruised off to whaling grounds around the world, and were later paid off and settled in New Bedford, Massachusetts, that an area in that town in the nineteenth century was known as Fayal.

At "Fredonia," the house of the American consul in Horta, where shipmasters, merchants, diplomats, and ocean-crossing VIPs dined and talked, the latest news of global affairs was heard first, in the age before sub-ocean telegraph cables, and discussed over local and Madeira wines before being passed on to those waiting for it on the distant continents. Fayal later became a coal-bunkering depot for steamships, an outpost for cable stations, a refueling stop for transoceanic aircraft. But after World War II, when technology outgrew most needs for a mid-ocean stopover, Fayal lapsed into a sleepy state and turned in on itself. Its people farmed, fished, and still went whaling in small oar-powered boats, throwing handheld harpoons. It was little visited except by the infrequent yacht and its bold crew.

When Eric and Susan Hiscock stopped in Horta in 1968, there were three yachts in the harbor. When J. and I first passed through, there were perhaps fifty yachts in port. Now more than seven hundred call each year, and Horta does much for the visiting yachtsman. Making a profound first impression on the overripe, water-rationed sailor is the barrack-sized bathhouse right on the quay, kept clean and swabbed, with ancient, grandly scaled porcelain tubs and brass fixtures and oceans of hot water. Women of deeply indeterminate middle age, reeking of Old World domestic skills, meet the sailor as he staggers ashore on rocky legs and relieve him of his embarrassing laundry and return it so clean and sweet-smelling he doesn't recognize it.

The local tourist board hosts races for cruising boats, with prizes and parties for all competitors and dinner at the Estalgem Santa Cruz, an old fort and now swank hotel on the harbor, for the winners and their crews. (We were told the Santa Cruz was owned by the actor Raymond Burr, who supposedly wandered around the lobby in spectacular kaftans when in residence. Unfortunately, I never saw this.) When we were there, J. raced *Toad* with an all-female crew, and I joined a singlehander named Jeffrey, whom we'd met in Bermuda a few weeks earlier. J. and her crew did *Toad* proud, passing a number of newer, sleeker boats by superior sail handling. Jeffrey's boat was small and light and in the near-calm conditions on race day we managed to pass most of the fleet of larger boats, placing fifth overall, but first on handicap for our size. We got the big dinner and cases of local wine, but Jeffrey turned out to be a bum and sailed off while we weren't looking with my half of our grand prize: a load of provisions from local stores. J. and I were as chronically broke as ever and for a while I hoped Jeffrey would dine on botulism.

The Fayalese treated people off visiting boats in a way I had only read about in the older Hiscock books, when Eric and Susan had circumnavigated in the fifties and cruising sailors were a rarity in the world: they were adopted, taken in by locals, treated like movie stars. As J. and I walked and hitchhiked around Fayal, locals would pick us up and not let us go. They took us home and fed us, gave us picnics, and took us anywhere we wanted to go. They seemed terribly flattered that we had sailed all the way from America—at great peril, they were convinced—to visit their island. They went out of their way for us. Some of them even appeared to be cruising the roads looking for yachties to entertain.

They particularly liked to watch us eat their prized homemade sausages. They all made them, they all wanted us to eat the stuff by the yard. Not being great meat eaters, we did our diplomatic best, but sometimes this was difficult. This *choriço* seemed full of nothing but dense yellow fat, coagulated blood, and gristle. On one occasion, when we were being picnicked beside the road by a middle-aged couple whose car trunk just happened to be full of food in baskets, and my cheeks were bulging like Dizzy Gillespie's with a ghastly unswallowable accumulation of animal by-products, a car came along the road and as our hosts turned to look at it, I spewed my mouthful into a hydrangea bush. My host saw this, or the tail end of it, and I began to cough convulsively as a cover-up. It had been an accident, of course, something caught in my throat. The sweet man pounded my back to stop my coughing, then immediately cut another huge chunk of *chorço* and with tender solicitude actually opened my mouth like a dentist and popped it in. For him, I chewed it up and swallowed it with convincing relish, and washed it down with good bread and wine.

The heart of the visiting sailing community in Horta is the Café Sport on the stone-cobbled Rua Tenente leading up from the harbor. It was founded by Henrique Azevedo, who befriended the first few yachts that turned up in the forties and fifties, organizing their needs, their laundry, their provisioning, and this tradition is carried on by his son Peter and grandson José. The Café Sport is the place to go when you first arrive, to have a beer or a glass of wine and see who else is there, to pick up your mail, which the café will hold, and while pawing through the mail pile, to see who else is on the way. It's a club, your club, where even you are welcome. It doesn't matter if you come off a little boat like *Toad* or an absentee-CEO's superyacht carrying *Toad*'s weight in electronics and a platoon of blond, liveried crewmembers. All who fetch up at Fayal have sailed across at least a thousand miles of ocean, and it's the little boats that have slogged harder with fewer resources to get there. I have felt more at home aboard *Toad* in Horta than in most places.

The Azores are lovely islands to approach from the sea. Joshua Slocum's landfall here in 1895, on his way around the world single-handed aboard his famous *Spray*, was typical of most sailors' first sight of the islands at the end of a passage:

Early on the morning of July 20 I saw Pico looming above the clouds on the starboard bow. Lower lands burst forth as the sun burned away the morning fog, and island after island came into view. As I approached nearer, cultivated fields appeared. . . . Only those who have seen the Azores from the deck of a vessel realize the beauty of the mid-ocean picture.

Pico's cone, O Pico, is an unmissable beacon in the ocean, seventy-six hundred feet above sea level and shaped like Mount Fuji. It rises directly and steeply, almost as far from the ocean floor to the surface as it continues above: in the two-mile channel between Pico and São Jorge, there are depths over five thousand feet.

The islands are volcanic, with small craters, or *caldeiras* (also the Portuguese word for a ship's boiler), poking up all over the landscape. The coasts are edged in black rock and sand. The soil is rich, the climate mild, and the slopes between the high *caldeiras* and the sea are checkered with the small green fields of farms. Fayal is called the Blue Island for the thick blue hydrangeas that border all its fields and lanes like a lattice over the landscape, and this blue and green weave dotted with whitewashed houses and villages is thrilling to see as you approach it after days or weeks on a blue-upon-blue ocean. The effect was no less exciting for our two cats, Minou and Neptune, as we approached from the west on our first visit, three long weeks out of Bermuda. They crouched on deck astounded, goggle-eyed at the materializing land, noses quivering as we came under the island's lee, as if they had forgotten entirely about the pungent nonwatery world and were seeing it and smelling it for the first time.

J. and I spent many days walking and hitching all over Fayal. We bought eggs and fruit and vegetables from farmers and their wives. We went inside the lighthouse high over the sea on Punta da Ribeirinha. We climbed to the island's summit and looked down into the swampy *caldeira*. We looked over at Pico just four miles across the water, and we looked far out to sea at where we had come from and turned and looked in the direction we hoped to go.

At that time the islanders were still whaling in small, open, oar-powered whaleboats, putting out from the beach when the cry *"Baleia! Baleia!"* went up from the lookout stations ashore, rowing for long hours after spouting, breaching whales. They rowed right up to the whales' backs and threw handheld harpoons into them exactly as the whalers of New Bedford and Nantucket had done a hundred and fifty years before. On our bucolic walks high on Fayal we saw the whales and the boats putting out from shore and followed the long, slow chase.

One night just before we sailed away, J. and I rowed back to *Toad* a little drunk and very happy and I got out our rocket distress flares and began firing them off over the anchorage. Other boats followed and the sky over the harbor suddenly filled with a dazzling display of shell bursts and red and white parachute flares. We sailed away and a week later we were screaming foully at each other in the lee of Cape St. Vincent.

I remember all this in the cloudy dawn of June 27, twelve days, 1,123 miles out of Falmouth, as I sit in the cockpit with a cup of coffee, staring ahead over a smooth gray sea.

0630: LANDFALL. I can see Graciosa plainly on the horizon, about 30 miles away.

0725: I think I can see Pico—the tip—bearing 210 Magnetic, above all the clouds, far ahead. Definitely Pico's cone. A magnificent landmark.

1000: Light rain, buggering us about with usual wind shifts. We've been about 7 degrees W of our daily DR since we left England, so I'm concluding the compass has a westerly deviation of 7 deg.

1100: Glad I saw Graciosa and Pico earlier—now hidden by clouds and showers—or I'd be wondering about our landfall.

1200: Graciosa now about 10 miles SE, faint under rain cloud, though we are in sunshine. Can't see Pico or Fayal.

1400: Punta de Barca, Graciosa, is due E True, about 8 miles. Little patchwork farms high above the sheer drop at the coast. Lonely, impregnable looking island.

1500: Can now see Ponta dos Rosais, NW tip of São Jorge, fine on port bow; and a smudge of Fayal off to the SW.

1530: Fayal, Pico, São Jorge all well in view now—should be eyeball navigation from here on in. Fishermen in an open boat half a mile abeam, waving.

1600: Dolphins playing around the boat. Impossible not to believe they are welcoming me.

1830: Sunny now, clouds all gone away, water blue and flattened right out in here among the islands. Wonderful to come back to such a place, remembering it so well as I see it. Have identified lighthouse on Punta da Ribeirinha which J. and I visited, and Punta da Espalamaca, Guia, and the whole lay of the land above and around Horta. A little bittersweet. Wind right down, ghosting along.

2000: Bearings on Pico, Guia, and Ribeirinha light place us 8 miles out of Horta. Looks more like 2 in clear early evening. Frustrating.

2100: 4 miles to Horta. Getting darker. I hope to get in while there's some light and pick up a mooring instead of anchoring, but wind is getting lighter and lighter. An hour maybe.

2300: We're here. In. Probably rounded the breakwater at about 2230. The place is packed with yachts and couldn't find a mooring in the dark, so dropped the hook farther out where it's a little lumpy from my blessed E'ly which has carried Toad and me here from Mylor. Amazing to be here. Lots of thoughts and feelings. Glad to be in. Pleased to have done it on my own, but sad J. isn't here with me. Good time—for old Toad—12½ days. Vane has worked incredibly, I haven't steered once from Mylor until Horta breakwater. Arrived about this time of night 2 years ago, and hear the same sound from ashore, the sound that struck us so after coming from America and made us realize we had reached Europe: the whine of small motorbikes zooming along the edge of the harbor and down the shore road. Drinking a cup of tea and contemplating 8 hours sleep without waking 16 times.

Horta

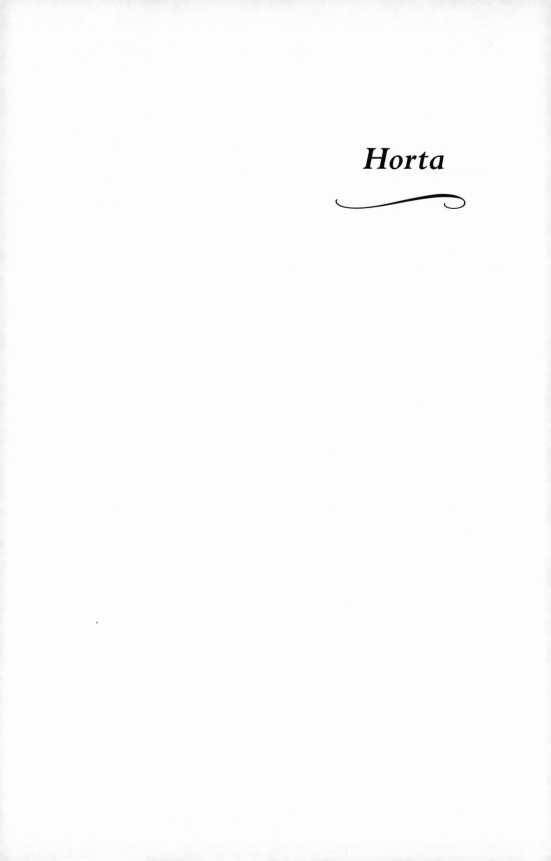

June 26

In the morning I row ashore and sign in with the maritime police at the *Capitania*, giving the name and displacement of my ship, the number of my crew, and the port of my destination. I receive a *Livrete de Transito de Embaracoes Estrangeiras*. I have my bath. I surrender my sailbag full of laundry to a stout woman who plants herself in front of me on the quay and simply takes it with a shy smile. I carry the twelve-volt battery that powers my stereo and VHF radio to a garage to be charged, and then I go up the Rua Tenente to the Café Sport. There's a letter from my mother congratulating me and telling me to call her. I use the phone at the Estalgem Santa Cruz, Raymond Burr's place.

"Are you lonely by yourself, baby?" my mother asks.

I try to tell her about the enjoyable loneliness I was starting to feel out at sea. Something like that elusive "oneness" that spiritual types are always banging on about. Like feeling as small as a plankton but part of an infinitely larger design. But I stop myself before I begin to sound sincerely enlightened and ask her how she's doing.

My mother is a painter and lives in a studio in London. This winter a man she was in love with, a sculptor, died of cancer. She hasn't talked about it much. With this event, I think she has begun to see herself as getting old. I bought her Gail Sheehy's book *Passages* a few months ago, which may not have been a tactful idea. She made a face and rolled her eyes when I gave it to her, and I don't think she's looked at it.

"I'm fine," she says. "Busy." Busy is good.

After hanging up, I look around the hotel for a girl I saw working here two years ago. Out at sea, remembering Horta, I suddenly remembered her. I never spoke to her, except to ask to use the phone. Two years later I still remember her face, and those eyes.

During the last year in London, newly single, I have found myself as awkward as a spotty adolescent in my few attempts to approach women. Nevertheless, I'm emboldened by my new image of myself as a man who has sailed alone across a thousand miles of ocean, and now I plan to come in, talk to this girl on some pretext, tell her I remember her, and, if I see any flicker of response, ask her out to dinner.

She's not here, though. I don't see Raymond Burr in a kaftan either.

I go for a walk, the thing I am dying to do when I come ashore after a passage at sea. I walk along the shore road out of town, past the beach and up the hill to Punta da Espalamaca, the prominent headland I steered for coming in. From here you can see all of Horta and the harbor and southeastern Fayal stretching away below you, and you can look across the four-mile channel of current-ripped water at Pico soaring to its Fujiyama cone, as J. and I did many times walking up this road and down the other side to the fishing and whaling villages of Praia and Pedro Miguel.

Suddenly, without warning, I am stabbed by a devastating lone-liness. It comes in under my rib cage and moves upward and crushes my heart. It comes on like a fit, squeezing me breathless, wringing me out, then eases, draining me away with it, leaving me undone, elaborate fortifications smashed. Oh boy. Is this what singlehanding is all about? I felt nothing remotely approaching this out at sea. While I was sailing toward a destination, I felt for some reason that I'd be less lonely once I arrived.

I turn around and head back down the hill toward Horta. I start thinking about when I will leave.

The next day I run into Bob Silverman at the Café Sport. Bob, an American, and his wife sailed here, liked it, and now live year-round on Fayal, in a small farmhouse not far from Punta Espala-maca. I met him two years ago and bought his small *Cruising Guide to the Azores*, which he wrote and published himself. It's an endearing little book, printed by the local newspaper, *O Telegrafo*, soft-covered, held together with two staples, illustrated with maps that I guess are drawn by Bob, or perhaps by a local child, and what appear to be antique daguerreotypes of Azorean ports and views, in which, however, can also be seen modern fiberglass yachts. Two years ago it was the only yacht-oriented guide to the Azores, full of good local knowledge not found in official pilot books, and with five hundred yachts a year calling at the islands, it was a hot item at the Café Sport. Bob also does sail repair work at home and is caretaker for the few but increasing number of boats left in Horta over the winter.

We have a drink with people off two other boats, and Bob invites us all up to his house for drinks tomorrow, Sunday.

On the way back down to the harbor I buy Saturday's copy of *O Telegrafo* and find *Toad* listed as one of the recently arrived *Iates de Recreio*: "*335—TOAD, americano. Desloca 5 tons. e e tripulado pelo navegador solitario Peter Nichols. Procede de Falmouth em 13 dias e vai para Camden (Estados Unidos)."*

Another singlehander has also made Saturday's paper. On the same page runs the headline: "*NAVEGADOR SOLITARIO ENCONTRADO MORTO A BORDO DO SEU IATE.*" The story is short. A merchant ship spotted a twenty-seven-foot-long yacht drifting 160 miles southwest of Fayal. The Portuguese naval corvette *Jacinto Candido* picked up the yacht, *Mariner*, and towed it to Fayal. The *iatista solitario*, Mark Spring, an Englishman, was found in the cabin, emaciated and dead.

Mariner, a small boat about the same size as *Toad*, is now bobbing at a mooring a hundred yards in front of me as I read this. It looks as if it has just floated in out of the Twilight Zone. The sails are tattered, lines hang off the deck and dangle in the water; it has a look of decay and abandonment I've never seen on another floating boat. The story running around the anchorage is that the boat was becalmed (I don't know if it had an engine or insufficient fuel) until the *iatista solitario* ran out of food and starved to death. A horrifying story, but it seems unlikely to me. Calms don't last that long, except in *The Rime of the Ancient Mariner*. In seven years of engineless cruising, three days is the longest calm I've known. *Mariner* is a lighter, newer boat than *Toad*, and probably a better sailor; making port should not have been a problem. The more likely explanation for such an awful end—worse, I think, than falling overboard—is that some accident or sickness incapacitated or killed him.

Sailors in mid-ocean are clearly vulnerable to physical problems. Assembling proper medical supplies, including antibiotics, syringes, and a good medical book, is part of conscientious preparation for heading offshore. Toothache is probably the severest problem most sailors will encounter, but of course there is worse. In March 1960, Eric and Susan Hiscock were in one of the remoter stretches of the Pacific, between the Galapagos and the Gambier Islands in southern Polynesia, far from any shipping lanes, when Eric developed a pain in his stomach:

> It was during the early part of the trip that a nagging pain in the appropriate part of my abdomen, between navel and hip bone, suggested to me that I was developing appendicitis. Miserably I realized that there was nothing to be done, for it would have been a long, slow and rough business sailing back to the Galapagos, and there was no doctor on those islands. There was no point in telling Susan about my symptoms, but after a day or two I could no longer keep the horrid secret to myself.
>
> "I've got a pain in my tummy," I said eventually, "and I think it may be appendicitis."
>
> Susan did not appear to be as concerned as I thought she would be, and after I had pinpointed the spot she said:
>
> "Well, I've had a pain there, too, for the past few days and it can't possibly be appendicitis in my case, as I've had mine out."
>
> I felt tremendously relieved, and the final conclusion we came to was that it must be some form of poisoning, possibly due to the Wreck Bay water, even though we had boiled it, and slowly we both recovered.

Having a companion to see you through such a problem, what-ever the outcome, is a comfort. Alone, you have only your imagina-tion. Robin Knox-Johnston, the Englishman who, in 1968–9, sailed around the world singlehanded and nonstop, the first person to do so, had a similar scare. His diet throughout his voyage, on which he thrived, was an unrelieved mix of heavy English institutional fare: beef, pork, stews, curries, solid puddings, which he ate while listening to tapes of Gilbert and Sullivan operettas. But on sev-eral occasions he developed severe indigestion, and one of these scared him:

> The indigestion developed until I had a permanent pain in the middle of my stomach. I got out my *Ship Captain's Medical Guide* and by the time I had finished looking up my symptoms and the possible causes, I was really alarmed. It appeared that I could have anything from appendicitis to stomach ulcers. I put myself on a diet of spaghetti cheese and rice puddings, which was most unsatisfying, but it did ease things a bit. I also started taking indigestion tablets, but the pain remained despite all this. Then its source appeared to shift and I got really scared. I took out the charts and measured off to the nearest decent-sized port, Belém, at the mouth of the Amazon, which was about a thou-sand miles away. That was at least ten days sailing, and in ten days if I did have appendicitis without any antibiotics aboard to keep the thing in check, I would be dead. I cursed myself for leaving antibiotics off my medical list, and for not having my appendix out before I set sail.

On his "improved" diet, Knox-Johnston got better. "I think I can, in retrospect, diagnose my trouble as a combination of chronic indigestion and acute imagination, and it shows the dangers of giving a layman a medical book!"

The danger from appendicitis for a sailor far from land is not what it once was. Antibiotics can in most cases control the infection for weeks until port is made, or clear it up altogether. However, many scientists tell us we are now at the dusk of the antibiotic age, that at some point in the near future mutating bacteria will circumvent the effects of antibiotics, and sailing far from land may become again the more perilous adventure it once was. The most frightening story I know of a singlehander confronting illness is what happened to Argentine Vito Dumas, who circumnavigated in 1942, in the preantibiotic age. His arm became so badly infected that he faced the prospect of amputating it himself.

That night must be the last with my arm in this condition. Land? I could not reach land in time. If by tomorrow things had not improved, I would have to amputate this useless arm, slung around my neck and already smelling of decay. It was dying and dragging me along with it. It was septicaemia. I could not give in without playing my last card. There were several suppurating open wounds . . . but I could not localize the septic focus in this formless mass. With an axe, or my seaman's knife, at the elbow, at the shoulder, I knew not where or how, somehow I would have to amputate.

Stephen King could not have laid out his predicament more gruesomely. But Dumas was spared the horror of self-amputation. He fell into fevered unconsciousness and woke later with the arm half its former size, his bunk awash in pus, the crisis past.

Sailors have discussed, as Knox-Johnston mentions, having an asymptomatic appendix removed before going to sea. I'm sure this has been done, and it's a routine operation, but I know of one case in which a young man planning to cruise the Pacific had his appendix preemptively removed and died of infection as a result of the operation.

You hear stories from other boaters, read them in the yachting press: a diabetic's insulin becomes spoiled in the heat of the tropics, and he dies a few days later; a young singlehander with a hitherto unsuspected heart condition is found dead in his boat north of the

Caribbean. Singlehanders can have strokes, fall and bang their heads, break limbs, wound and puncture themselves, and then they must look to themselves and some book for a doctor.

What happened to Mark Spring remains, for me, a mystery. Illness, or accident, or, possibly, incompetence killed him. There are people who go to sea unable to navigate. I've met them, and listened to them telling me how they radioed passing ships for directions, and the angel of nincompoops watches over them. But I would not blame the sea for anyone's death, any more than I would blame a road, even an icy road with a sharp curve, for an accident: it's up to the driver to approach it accordingly.

Poor unkempt *Mariner* is a sad sight.

July 3

Klaus Alverman is one of the group that meets at the Café Sport Sunday morning to walk up to Bob's house. Klaus built his pretty twenty-six-foot cutter *Plumbelly of Bequia* on the beach at Bequia, in the West Indies, out of local wood and materials, with the advice and assistance of local boatbuilders, and then sailed it, without an engine, around the world. I've heard about him from Ed Boden, the limerick-babbling rocket engineer, who circumnavigated at about the same time. *Plumbelly* has no standing headroom, and Klaus is about six feet three inches tall. He's dressed in neat slacks and a shirt and looks like a banker on a weekend. He's on his way to Europe.

With Klaus and me are two American couples, both from unattractive fiberglass boats in the forty- to forty-five-foot range, featuring all modern conveniences, Buicks of the sea. We walk up a cobbled road into the countryside above town.

The houses everywhere on the island are built of black volcanic blocks, usually plastered and whitewashed, their windows painted with broad borders of a blue that goes well with the hydrangeas always nearby. Bob and his wife live in a low farmhouse, the walls of most of its small rooms knocked down, making it spacious and bright inside with a farmhouse kitchen that runs into the living room and large windows giving views across farmland down to Horta and the harbor and Pico across the water. It's exactly the sort of island house I would want to live in if I couldn't live aboard a boat. We have beer and wine and a local goat's-milk cheese very like Spanish Manchego, and talk, as boaters incessantly do, about boats and their gear.

On the way back down to town a few hours later, I remark how much I like Bob's house and what a great life he and his wife have made for themselves here. They have a nice home, live in a community where there's an abundance of inexpensive fresh local produce of every sort, and have as much contact as they wish with people sailing through from all parts of the world. One of the American women, Gail, turns and looks at me as if I've just farted.

"But to *live* here? With these people?" she says. "That poor woman."

"What do you mean? You don't think she likes it here? What about these people?"

"Peter, they're peasants. She's an American. She's miserable."

"Really?" I'm amazed. "What did she say?"

"She didn't have to say anything."

Maybe she's right. But now I know how Gail and her husband can be happy aboard their horrible plastic boat with its big windows and ten jerry jugs tied to the rails down each side, and a profile that's against nature. "It should be at the bottom of the sea immediately," Mike Underhill, my literate hermit friend who lived in a tin shack on Tortola, used to say of such boats.

Gail's remarks bother me. I don't believe Bob's wife is unhappy. But I start thinking about isolation, and back aboard *Toad*, looking around my little home, it's Klaus's face that appears before me and disturbs me. He seemed aloof and unengaged up at Bob's house. Although polite and pleasant, he appeared to derive little joy from the company. I wonder why he came with us, particularly as Bob didn't give us lunch.

I begin to wonder if after years alone at sea, with short jumps ashore, Klaus has lost the knack of being with people. Maybe he tagged along with us out of a sense that when ashore that's what you do. The idea frightens me. I know I'm projecting my state of mind onto Klaus. He may be perfectly happy, but I'm still feeling terribly lonely in Horta, far more so here, surrounded by people, than out at sea alone. Already I want to set sail again as soon as possible. I can see myself turning into what I'm now imagining Klaus to be: an oceanic satellite, circling the earth at four knots, the ultimate example of Robert Louis Stevenson's notion that traveling hopefully is better than arriving. Leaving could grow better than staying. There is much I find attractive in the idea—that sort of self-sufficiency is anyway a big part of the attraction of cruising in a sailboat—but I see that I could sail too far, perhaps, and not come altogether back.

Or I might turn into Wilfred, from Mylor, another specter of what I'm afraid I could become as a singlehander, a nautical hermit crab aground in some backwater, seedy, reduced, unloved.

Or perhaps not. I'm alone. I miss J. terribly, particularly here where we were so close and had so much fun together. I want to connect, as E. M. Forster put it, and I feel so disconnected. I've come away from the Silverman house warmed by the life Bob and his wife have made for themselves here. I envy them for it and for having each other.

Lying in a glass case in the Café Sport are sperm whale teeth, and oval sawn cross-sections of these teeth, etched with scrimshaw. Every time I go into the café I peer at them through the glass, as I would if they were displayed in a museum. And I've seen scrimshaw in the whaling museums in New Bedford and Nantucket and these seem to me to be of museum quality. Scenes of men in whaleboats, breaching sperm, square-rigged ships, accurate in form and scale, beautiful in composition, all minutely etched in these smooth round four- and five-inch teeth the color of the dense cream that sat unmixed at the top of milk bottles when I was a boy in England. They are all done by local scrimshander Othon Silveira, and they are all for sale. I would love to own a piece of scrimshaw, but these are far beyond my price range. However, as a distant second best, I ask where Othon lives and walk to his house on the west side of Horta, a short distance from the port, in hopes of seeing and photographing this artist at work.

Ever since I saw Azorean whaleboats two years ago and watched them set out from Fayal's beaches after spouting sperm in the Pico Channel, I have been fascinated by whaling—not the horror of factory whaling, but the Moby Dick kind: oar-propelled boats, hand-held harpoons. What I saw in Fayal that year (and it was the last year the Azoreans went whaling before a worldwide moratorium stopped them, probably forever) was an exact, unimproved living example of the method used by Yankee whalers of centuries past. I've read some books about whaling in the past two years, and I've grown to love the whaleman's art of scrimshaw. It seems to me the saltiest of all the sailorman's many and beautiful arts.

A year ago, sailing out of the Mediterranean on our way to England, J. and I stopped in the Spanish port of Motril, where I had a discussion about scrimshaw with another yachtie, an American named Whit, who was headed east into the Mediterranean with his wife. Whit was morally perturbed by the issue of scrimshaw. He became surly and said that it was scrimshaw lovers like me who perpetrated the slaughter of whales. I told him that while I deplored the killing of whales by anybody on any scale, I didn't think the Azoreans did it to pull teeth to sell to tourists, but that scrimshaw was simply a utilization of an otherwise useless whale by-product, and beautiful and historically interesting. However, Whit grew angry with me and my atavistic rationalizations, and I thought: *You self-righteous jerk; look at the petroleum-derived dacron lines and sails all over your nonbiodegradable fiberglass boat, which itself will find its most lasting incarnation as landfill to offend humans and maggots for a thousand years; these aren't by-products of the automobile industry; people are polluting the world and rendering life on earth untenable just for you.*

Othon is middle-aged and lives with his mother. His studio is in the basement. Like every Azorean I've met, he has a sweet, open appreciation of any foreign sailors who make their way to his door. When I arrive, a German couple off another boat is already there, buying up whole pounds of scrimshaw. There's an air of rapacious glee about them, as if they know they're paying far less than the pieces are worth in the outside world, and are dying to sail away and tell everyone they ever meet what a great deal they made for themselves. They're dealing with Othon as if he were an uneducated

Bantu holding an armful of elephant ivory. I say hello and tell him I just wanted to see what he did, and maybe photograph some pieces, but I can come back another time. I am obviously not a paying customer, but Othon takes the time to gather some fine pieces and a strip of black velvet and tells me to take everything outside and photograph the scrimshaw on the velvet in daylight.

The Germans pass me outside on their way out, squealing and guffawing, hurrying, with their eyes down.

Back in Othon's studio, I talk to him while he cuts an oval cross-section of a large sperm whale tooth and polishes the flat sides smooth on an electric buffing wheel. I photograph him working as we talk about scrimshaw, whaling, the moratorium, and about sailing. He asks me chattily if I have a photograph of my boat. I do: in my wallet I carry a picture I took of J. sailing *Toad* in the cruisers' race in the Pico Channel two years ago. I show it to him. Othon now covers one side of the tooth section with black waterproof ink and begins to scratch away at the tooth through the ink. For this he uses a thick carbide-tipped needle held in something like an X-Acto knife. Gradually a white-negative scene evolves on the black-inked side of the whale tooth—I'm stunned when I see that Othon is drawing *Toad*: its bowsprit, bobstay, boom gallows all there in the proportions I know so well, three sails filled, a little figure—J.—at the helm, a billowing cloud rising behind the sails, small choppy waves in the foreground. All this in an oval shape an inch by inch and a quarter, with about a quarter of an inch of untouched black surrounding the scene.

"What is your boat's name?" asks Othon.

"*Toad*," I say, feeling my heart wanting to burst.

Othon has me spell it out as he engraves the letters between inverted commas at the bottom of the scene on the tooth. Then he covers the whole side again with black ink. In a moment it dries and he takes it to the buffing wheel. All the ink is polished off, except the ink in the etched lines, and there is *Toad* with J. at the helm in the Pico Channel scrimshanded on a creamy section of sperm whale tooth. Othon hands it to me.

I don't know how to word a sufficient thank-you, but he seems to know what I'm feeling and he smiles and looks almost as happy as I am.

Back aboard *Toad*, rocking a little in the anchorage, I look at my priceless and personal piece of scrimshaw and wonder what to do with it. Finally, I decide to use it as I imagine a Yankee whaleman might have: I drill a small careful hole in the top of the scene, above *Toad*'s mast. I run a piece of tarred marlin twine through the hole, knot it, and pull it over my head. My scrimshaw hangs around my neck.

It hangs around my neck now as I write.

Here in Horta, when my thoughts aren't tortuously tied up with J., they tend to turn in the direction of other women.

There's a red boat in the anchorage called *Jeshan*, a hard-chine steel cutter. I've heard that it has been built by a woman and sailed halfway around the world, from Australia, by her alone. This is unusual: there are far fewer women than men in the pantheon of singlehanders, and at sea in general. Britain's Naomi James—subsequently Dame Naomi—circumnavigated alone, with only one stop, in South Africa; American Tania Aebi circumnavigated in a boat smaller than *Toad*, setting off while she was still a teenager. Ann Gash, the "sailing granny" from Australia, sailed alone most of the way around the world; Isabelle Autissier and Florence Arthaud, both from France, are formidable competitors in long-distance grand prix singlehanded events. And there are others, but these women are a minority in a statistically male-dominated field. Yet there's no good reason for this; physically, women are just as capable as men aboard a boat. Mentally, I imagine, they would be stronger and more tenacious. Yet there is an initial self-conscious, self-aggrandizing boldness of intent in sailing across an ocean alone and this may be more of a male trait—it has the smack of machismo about it.

A female singlehander, therefore, would be someone I'd like to meet. Perhaps she and I would run into each other again, in more distant ports. Already I can see us in the South Pacific, waving at each other across half a mile of ocean as we raise the palms on Aitutaki. But every time I row past *Jeshan* on my way to or from shore, there are at least five other dinghies tied to its stern and a large band of men surrounding the blonde in the cockpit. I row on.*

On several evenings I go eat at a small hole-in-the-wall café off the Praça do Infante where J. and I used to go. The food is dirt cheap and not very good, but it's frequented by other boaters and I go there in hopes of talking with someone. One evening I meet three Germans there, a young man and two girls, tourists without boats, which is unusual in Horta. They're intrigued by the cruising life and I invite them out to see *Toad*. I quickly figure out who's with whom and begin to get hopeful about the other girl.

We walk down to the harbor and pile into my dinghy. This is a small sailing dinghy, with a centerboard case. As I row us away from shore, I see that the weight of the four of us (the girls are large bovine German girls) has lowered the top of the centerboard case until it's below the surrounding sea level: water is flooding in over the case. I try to get my passengers to bail with the bottomless plastic bleach bottle I use as bailer, but they're unaware of the sudden urgency of the situation, and I don't want to frighten them by shouting at them to bail for all they're worth. I turn the dinghy around and head back toward shore, but we are still well out in the anchorage. As water comes in, the weight in the boat increases and the situation deteriorates with exponential speed. The end comes

*The woman was Julia Hazel, and later I recognized her and her boat when she started writing articles for *Cruising World* magazine. Julia went on around the other half of the world and completed her circumnavigation by herself.

abruptly as the gunwales reach sea level and water pours over the top and the dinghy disappears beneath us. The water is cold; we all gasp. The Germans are completely surprised, but even treading water they remain polite and good-natured, and still defer to me as the nautical authority. They ask me what we should do. I suggest swimming ashore. Fortunately they can all swim. The dinghy, which has some flotation built into its seats, reappears half-submerged back on the surface and I tow it after me, following my guests ashore.

The Germans walk out of the water shivering and laughing, and thanking me for such a great adventure. Their suspicions of the perilous nature of small-boat sailing are confirmed. There are some jokes about how I've made it this far from England. They decide to go back to their hotel and change. We say good night.

I think it's time to head for Maine.

Fayal to 36°08' North; 53°12' West

July 8

1035: Well. What a night. Long story short—I realized at 0200 when I had to pump out for about 2 minutes, after things had long since calmed down, that we were taking on far too much water. I think I've located the main source: the planking up forward. I watched it flexing on each wave, and saw water coming in both sides of the stem. I spent the entire night, from 0200 until 1000 this morning, sawing up some spare plywood and fitting additional floor timbers. They're pretty flimsy, but hopefully now the boat won't actually break up, or if it does, it won't go real fast. I must now, however, be seriously prepared to abandon Toad—

As I write this the pen stops moving. I get up and make another cup of coffee and what I've just written reverberates around my mind like a sound in a canyon: loud then faint then loud again. Coffee ready, I take my mug back to the saloon table and start writing in the log again.

I won't, unless it actually sinks. I don't mind pumping a lot, I just hope it doesn't get a lot worse, as it began to do yesterday after a not at all severe day of beating to windward. (We're beating now, but more gently.) I thought about going back to the Azores, but what could I do to the boat there? I have no money to fix it properly. I probably couldn't get any work in Fayal. Going on to Europe isn't really any different than continuing on to the States, where at least I can get work, and anyway I don't want to go back to Europe. So, I'll pump and head for Bermuda. If we're still in reasonable shape by the time we near Bermuda, I'll head for Maine. Sail it straight in to some yard in Camden, haul it out and live aboard, find work, get money, make repairs. Launch. Sail around the world. Sounds good. Maybe it's mad to carry on. I hope not.

1315: Noon pos: 32°52'N, 32°08'W. A measly 49 miles made good to the SW from yesterday's position. 446 since leaving Horta 6 days ago. Over 2000 to go.

After writing up the log I have lunch. Azorean cabbage, my bread, a tin of smoked oysters. It's the first time I've relaxed since last night. The sun is out. It's pleasant. Get a grip.

Most traditionally built wooden boats take on water, particularly when driven hard. Their hulls flex, and water finds its way in. They leak when they're first launched after they are built. They leak after a winter ashore, during which their planks and timbers dry out and shrink and require a period of immersion for the wood to swell up and become watertight again. They leak when putting to sea after a long period of idleness. They leak sitting still.

Toad has always leaked. When we beat across the Anegada Passage from the Virgins to St. Barts, and across the Florida Straits to the Bahamas after months in the anchorage off Dinner Key, and when we thrashed through one long and desperate night against a *levante* gale blowing out of the Straits of Gilbraltar as we tried to get into the Mediterranean, water had sloshed in the bilge and required long minutes of pumping to get rid of. But when the hard chance was past, and the stress on the hull gone, the water has always stopped coming in.

Not so now. We've been beating, but not hard, into a west-southwesterly wind and some short but steep waves for the last 2 days, July 6 and 7. This morning the wind veered to the northwest and dropped and *Toad* is once again plodding along in the gentlest of conditions, and water is still coming in.

I know *Toad*, and all its timbers and its every component, as I have known nothing else, and I know something is changed and wrong. I can't actually believe the trouble is some weakness in the hull, and my night-long work banging in extra floor timbers was, now that I think about it, an unthinking reaction to seeing water coming in up forward. It hasn't stopped the leaking. It has only re-assured me that the bow isn't going to crumble inward.

In the last five years I have built over eighty doubler, or "sister," frames into the hull—laminating thin strips of douglas fir and epoxy glue alongside the older, original frames on the inside of the planking until the desired thickness was reached, then fastening them in place through the outside of the hull planking with hundreds of bronze screws—effectively doubling the skeletal strength of the hull. Until today I've believed that *Toad* was at least as strong as when it was built, in 1939. There is no rot in the boat. When J. and I "wooded" the hull between deck and waterline, sanding down through decades of paint to the bare planking before repainting, the larch looked and smelled like new wood, and in places still dribbled resinous sap. My night of panicked carpentry over, I still have to believe that *Toad* is fundamentally sound. It's got to be something else.

In England, ten years ago, *Toad*'s previous owner, a Dutchman called Henry, sheathed the hull from the waterline down with a nylon cloth sold under the brand name Cascover. He did this as a precaution against the teredo, or shipworm, an almost invisible organism that lives in seawater and likes to bore into the planks of wooden boats, whereupon it grows into a worm with sharp wood-cutting teeth at one end. In the tropics, where Henry was taking the boat, the teredo can grow as long as six feet. It then eats its way through the boat's planking. Reading descriptions of the teredo, I've always imagined a 1950s horror movie scene of the luckless yachtsman being taken unawares by a giant python-sized, incisor-gnashing worm bursting through the planking one night as he sits drinking his cocoa and listening to the BBC. In fact, the worm stays within the wood and doesn't grow larger than spaghetti. But the damage it can do to a boat is scary enough, turning whole planks into papier-mâché. Good bottom paint, thickly applied, will keep worms out, but paint can be scraped off during accidental groundings, or the impecunious yachtsman may let it go too long between repainting. Hull sheathing of some form is better. For hundreds of years, wooden ships, and many yachts, were sheathed with thin copper sheets, which not only prevented worm attacks, but kept the bottom clean by leaching cuprous oxide, which is toxic to marine flora that will adhere to anything in the water and grow into slimy weed. Fiberglass is a modern alternative, but the glass and polyester resin matrix doesn't stick well to the flexing hulls of traditionally built boats. It is better stuck onto stiff plywood or modern cold-molded boats, and then with the more expensive but stronger and more waterproof epoxy resin.

Cascover was developed as a deck covering. I don't know if the manufacturers recommended it for hull sheathing below the waterline, where it would be constantly submerged, but Henry put it on, glued to the wood with resorcinol glue. It has lasted ten years, but I've never liked the idea of it. Resorcinol glue can become brittle with age, unlike epoxy, which is somewhat elastic. Before leaving Mylor, I noticed that some of the sheathing below the waterline was delaminating, coming away from the hull. I believed this was the source of some of the water that periodically leaked into *Toad*'s bilge, and I glued it back onto the hull with epoxy resin. But I'm unhappy about the rest of it. I've decided to take the sheathing entirely off the hull when I get to Maine, and try something else, either just good antifouling paint or cold-molding the hull with thin laminations of wood veneer and epoxy. But it has worked for ten years, I reasoned back in Mylor, it will surely last another two or three months until I get to Maine.

Maybe. If that's the problem. I have to find out.

We're moving along at between two and three knots. I get out my mask and snorkel and go forward and sit on the bowsprit. I look around for sharks and don't see any. As if I'd see any. I put on the mask and snorkel, tie a line around my waist, and climb down onto the bobstay, the chain that runs from the tip of the bowsprit to an eyebolt in the stem just above the waterline. It's the best place to sit when the dolphins are zeroing in on our bow wave, zigzagging back and forth in front of the boat. I look around once more, then drop into the water, keeping a good hold on the chain. I look back down along the stem and along the hull on each side. My repair to the sheathing looks fine. The rest of the sheathing looks good, no signs of any delamination.

Then, just for a moment, I look down into the ocean. It looks like blue fog, with refracted bolts of light stabbing down into its depths. *Toad* hovers, levitated somehow, in a pocket of water that is oddly clear and uncolored by the surrounding blue. I look around horizontally and see nothing but blue. I feel an incredible, visceral, unreasoning fear of the depths below me, the limitless water around me, of what might suddenly materialize streaking toward me out of the diaphanous blue. I remember how Robin Knox-Johnston spent hours in the water repairing a leaky seam in his wooden boat *Suhaili*, and I force myself to hang on to the bobstay for a moment longer. And then I can't, not for another nanosecond, and I'm clawing up the bobstay over the bowsprit onto the deck, where I stand dripping and gasping.

Back inside the boat, water is still, and now, quite mysteriously, trickling in, pooling in the bilge, rising. I pump it out again.

I spend the afternoon preparing a ditch bag of essentials I will grab if *Toad* goes down fast and I have to take to the dinghy in a hurry: fishing gear, some food (including my Neal's Yard peanut butter, which I've barely touched since leaving England but for some reason now strikes me as essential survival food), water, passport, sextant, watch, almanac and tables, sunblock, hat, Swiss army knife, rocket flares, and *The Decline and Fall of the Roman Empire* by Edward Gibbon, which, like my peanut butter, I've been having some trouble getting into. Perhaps, facing imminent death in a tiny dinghy bobbing on the ocean's surface, both book and peanut butter will at last prove to be richly sustaining.

I don't have a proper inflatable life raft aboard *Toad*. I couldn't afford one, and since I've read many accounts of life rafts failing to inflate when launched, or falling apart soon afterward, I don't feel too badly about this. Stowed underneath *Toad*'s cockpit is our old, patched inflatable dinghy, but I don't plan on launching that and sitting in it until I die. My plan, if I really have to abandon ship, is to get into my eight-foot sailing dinghy, with its positive flotation, and step its mast, raise its sail, and go. I don't expect to encounter really bad weather. I can bail out the waves that slop in. I can heave-to and sleep. I will read about dissolute Romans when becalmed. Most importantly, I can move toward a destination, without waiting for someone to spot me in the middle of the ocean (something ships have proven notoriously unable to do when passing life rafts full of frenziedly waving castaways). I'll head either for Bermuda or the Azores, depending on which is closer. I know the ability to carry on will help me psychologically.

The weather—which at no time has been bad, although we've just had several days of gray skies, lumpy seas, and wind from ahead—turns pleasant again.

This evening we move along over a flat sea at about three knots, straight toward the setting sun. Life aboard *Toad* is as nice as it has ever been. I listen to Meredith D'Ambrosio's piano on the Voice of America's Jazz Hour, hosted by the smoky-voiced Willis Conover. A great dinner comes out of the pressure cooker: a many-bean mix with tomatoes, onions, garlic, herbs, and various Azorean vegetables. I drink Azorean wine. I watch the sun go down on the flat horizon ahead and see the green flash. All the time I wonder if I'll have to abandon *Toad*.

July 9

Two minutes' pumping every two hours clears the bilge. Water seems to be coming in at a steady rate; fine if that rate holds. The weather today is still gentle and nothing seems amiss aboard *Toad*. But since considering the possibility of the boat sinking, I have wondered how I would confront J. with this loss and what she would think. Will it appear to be my fault? Will she be disgusted with me? Will she hate me? Will that make it really the end? Even though I'm sailing *Toad* to the States to sell it, it is more than just property to both of us. More like a child that we are putting up for adoption, and we are going through the motions despite deeply ambivalent feelings. After all we went through together aboard this boat, it still seems unthinkable to get rid of it, just as it still seems so odd to me at moments throughout every day that J. is not aboard. While *Toad* is afloat, I have always thought we might get back together.

This thought always brings up the questions I continue to ask myself about what went wrong with us. And these questions pull me irresistibly to her diaries—now that I've opened the bag and found them—to pore through them in a queasy reverie of nostalgia and pain.

In the late fall, after almost six months in the south of France, *Viva III* was sold. J. had grown happier, particularly through September and October when the mobs had left the coast and we had been there so long and knew it so well that we felt like residents. She had come to think of *Viva* as her home, and it wrenched her to leave.

Grimly, we emptied out the boat and drove back to England. Somewhere in farm country in northern France—she writes and I remember now, though I had forgotten—we picked up a load of delicious white beets spilled beside the road and ate them for days afterward.

J. grew very depressed in London. I think sharing me again with her brother and my family after six months alone together on the boat, seeing me able and eager to amuse myself with others, made her feel rejected. Nothing I could say or do made any difference—except not seeing David or Martin or my mother. She would have been happier, I felt, if we were marooned on a desert island together. This scared me. Entry after entry in her diary records that she is unhappy, depressed, that we fight. The more depressed she became, the easier I found it to be elsewhere.

I remember this; it is the degree I had forgotten. But it's all here in the unrelenting ledger of her unhappiness, in a tight imploding hand. I flip quickly past many pages detailing her disappointment with me—written almost as appeals. Or were they written for me to read? If I had been the diarist, she would certainly have ferreted out and read everything I wrote. These diaries lay around for years, but I never opened them until now. Was I meant to?

At Christmas we went to the Virgin Islands with Martin, his girlfriend, and J.'s and Martin's father and stepmother. It was no longer my turf, as J. saw London, and she was happier. It was beautiful and there were boats everywhere. We decided we wanted to live on a boat again, so we planned that Christmas to move to the Virgins as soon as we could and somehow find a boat. She was thrilled to leave London, and it was clear to me that things were not going well for us there. Somewhere new might help us.

We spent spring in Washington, D.C., living at her father's house in Georgetown, making money for our move. I drove a Red Top cab, nights mostly, out of Arlington, and J. worked in a Georgetown boutique.

Suddenly her diary presents me with a record of events I had no idea of. José, her old Bolivian boyfriend, was evidently in Washington also, and they began to see each other. At a bar called Charing Cross, at other unnamed places, and, at least once, they drove out to Great Falls and picnicked. She continued to see him over a period of many weeks, after work, while I drove my cab over in Virginia, across the Potomac. She writes that these meetings are fun, relaxed, that he is his old, warm self, that she feels good with him. She also writes that she and I bring out the worst in each other, that we depress each other, that she wonders what we're doing together.

I'm a little stunned, after all this time, to read this now. I remember now her telling me often that she was going out after work with Cindy, the girl she worked with in the boutique. Cindy and J. did become friends, and they did go out together, but obviously a little less than I knew.

I wonder what she and José did together—the diary is uncharacteristically vague. I wonder if she thought of leaving me and going off with him. Did she want to, and he didn't? How close was it for her? Why did she stay with me?

Because she did. Our plans went ahead. In March we flew to St. Thomas and ferried on to Tortola, in the British Virgins. After a few days in a guest house in Road Town, hitchhiking around the island to look at apartments and little houses, we rented an apartment on Frenchman's Cay in West End. This was a sleepy place then. There was one bar, Poor Richard's, run by Rick, a hospitable but enigmatic American who was circumspect with details of his past, and his present existence when not behind his bar. There were no charter boats there, only local fishing boats and a few small wooden yachts anchored out in the blue ten-fathom deep of the bay.

Suddenly we were happy. J.'s diary changes immediately, in tone and to look at: the pages are no longer empty save for a tortured comment or a complaint about P. They are filled, in a larger, more confident hand, with accounts of our life together. We walked and hitchhiked all over the island, exploring, swimming, looking at boats. We met English ex-pats living on Tortola who gave us rides and sometimes knew of boats for sale.

We fell in love with Tortola. I remember it now, at least during our earliest days there, as an unspoiled Caribbean island, deserted by all but its indigenous natives. Perhaps it was the season, or perhaps because we were always on foot and made our own paths over the island and were as shy as pandas in avoiding all signs of civilization, we seemed to find only empty beaches and an untrodden landscape. We stumbled dry-mouthed out of the hills into corrugated-tin-roofed native settlements, found the wooden shack that passed for a village store, and bought icy bottles of Malta, a sweet nonalcoholic malt drink that neither of us had ever tasted before. For all we saw of any sign of tourism it might have been the 1940s. I carried a machete on our treks, and sometimes, like Stewart Granger in a cheesy old safari movie, I actually hacked paths for us through the scrub. I sliced open wild papayas for my woman to eat and shinnied up coconut trees for young nuts and chopped their tops off so we could drink the milk. It felt like remotest Polynesia, and as we explored we chattered about boats and where we would someday sail in one.

We met Mike Underhill, an Englishman who lived with his two children, Sally, fifteen, and Ian, twelve, in a corrugated tin shack hidden in the trees above West End. Mike was bald and looked like the actor Robert Duvall. At home he never wore anything except brief swimming trunks; outside he would add a shirt and cap. The two kids were dark, straight-haired, and beautiful; their mother was from British Guiana, lived in Road Town, and visited the family infrequently. Mike dove for crayfish, which he sold to Rick at Poor Richard's and to others. This was his primary source of income, although he also had a well-equipped metalworking shop, including a large lathe, in one half of his living room, and he did repairs for the odd boater who somehow found him. He was intelligent, had thousands of books stacked everywhere, was seriously well-read, had a great sense of humor, and had a full-blown paranoia concerning the local natives. He was always sure several of them were lurking in the brush nearby intent on stealing something, and he kept a number of loaded guns stuffed under the cushions of his decrepit drawing room suite. He was reserved when we first met him, but after several weeks he eased up. We spent hours in his shack talking with him. Over our three years in the Virgins he became a great friend. He lent me books and taught me to hyperventilate before diving.

April 23 was our first wedding anniversary. We visited Mike, then put on good clothes and hitched into Road Town, where we had a beer at the Moorings, dinner at the Fort Burt Hotel overlooking Road Harbor, and danced to a steel band, which, J. writes, even I enjoyed.

We learned of an interesting boat for sale in St. Thomas and took the ferry over to look at it: *Fomalhaut*, a thirty-six-foot, plumb-bowed cutter designed by Sam Crocker, built in 1939 by the now-famous Bud McIntosh in New Hampshire. We saw her alongside the dock at Antilles Yacht Services, a boatyard in a mangrove-encircled inlet on the southeast side of the island, known to locals as "the Lagoon." It was a place we would come to know too well. We liked the boat right away, we thought she was beautiful, we saw ourselves living aboard her. So we were disappointed to hear from Billy Walker, the boatyard's resident shipwright, that *Fomalhaut* was in poor structural condition, that it would require a long time and too much money to put her in shape. In addition to much else, she needed complete "refastening," he said, and we didn't know what that meant. "It means replacing every screw in the hull," said Billy. Bummed, we took the ferry back to Tortola.

It was clear to us that to find a boat we would have to move to St. Thomas. We'd seen everything in Tortola, and there were at least ten times as many boats in St. Thomas. We even had a place to go. At the boatyard in the Lagoon, we had met and talked with Newt Farley, a marine surveyor who lived aboard his own boat, *Xanadu*, in Red Hook on the east end of St. Thomas. He had offered to let us stay aboard the boat in return for doing some varnish work. That sounded a little too cozy until he told us that *Xanadu* was a 110-foot-long steam yacht and we'd have our own suite.

But we were reluctant to leave Tortola. We hung on for a couple of weeks, and then our impossible fantasy-island existence came to an abrupt, ignominious end. Tortola's immigration officials, imperious and intractable as sultans (the tiresome colonial legacy in all the formerly British islands of the Caribbean), refused to extend our visas, and we were given one day to pack up and leave the British Virgin Islands. We had been there just a month.

I phoned Newt Farley, who again offered us room and board for a little work on his boat, and we packed up hurriedly in a day and took the ferry to St. Thomas. We bused to Red Hook, where *Xanadu* lay at anchor, arriving in the tropical twilight. We met Newt on the dock at Johnny Harms's sportfishing marina, with his wife Deirdre, home from her day at work, and Bob, another *Xanadu* live-aboard. We all motored out to the great yacht in Newt's whaler.

It was much too fast for J. Her diary entry written that evening in our new stateroom has a frantic, bewildered tone. She felt desperate, cornered, and unprovided-for. . . .

It quickly became clear to us that living aboard *Xanadu* was only an uneasy stopgap arrangement. The boat was extraordinary. Built in Maine in 1915, formerly owned by J. P. Morgan, later a Vanderbilt, she had a long clipper bow, a bowsprit, a slender fantail stern, a tall funnel, and two masts, the aft a little taller, all raked at a slight angle that gave the ship even while sitting still an impression of graceful speed. She was a grand yacht, the most gorgeous I have ever been aboard. But her beauty came all from her lines and the echoes she gave off of the great period in which she had been built, for she was now run-down and owned by a dreamer who couldn't afford her insistent upkeep. Weed grew at the waterline ("Few things look more slovenly," Eric Hiscock has written sternly of this condition), the varnished teak, acres of it, blistered in the tropical sun, which dried out her deck and hull planking and caused her to leak like a sieve. Her steam engine was "temporarily" not working, and to go anywhere she had to be towed, but there was nowhere to go. She was a lovely relic from another world, useless in this one.

Living aboard her in desperate, cracked glamour were Newt, marine surveyor who knew too well the state of his boat, and Deirdre, the Mrs. Rochester of the high seas, although she didn't stay locked in a stateroom but went ashore every morning to work in a tourist boutique in downtown Charlotte Amalie. She would come home evenings with steaks bought not from the Pueblo supermarket where the peons shopped, she told us with manic disdain, but from Jerry's Meats, elitist purveyor of flown-in-direct-from-Texas meat who sold only to the best restaurants in St. Thomas, and to Deirdre Farley. We would dine like Vanderbilts in *Xanadu*'s mahogany-paneled dining room, while Deirdre would rant about the cruise-ship hoi polloi who had trekked through her shop that day. Later on, as every evening progressed, both she and Newt grew drunker and began to yell savage things at each other. Then J. and I would creep away, out onto the deck, or we'd take the whaler and go ashore, or we'd just slink down the banistered stairway to our paneled stateroom and try to read or comfort each other or plot our way out, while somewhere away through the bulkheads Newt and Deirdre shrieked and barked.

Bob, the other member of our shipboard family, was a large, cheerful, red-bearded man from Maine, living aboard under the same arrangement we were: food and a stateroom in return for some daily effort against the onslaught of *Xanadu*'s decay. He seemed perfectly happy aboard. He paid no attention to Newt and Deirdre's fights, but amused himself about the boat, taking small pumps, winches, and unimportant machinery apart, down to their minutest components, which he would lay out neatly and fondle with oil. These things, which required only a wrench and elbow grease, one could do aboard *Xanadu*. Basic repairs like fixing the huge antique engine, refastening and caulking the hull, repairing the rot, would have cost hundreds of thousands of dollars; millions would have been needed to bring her back to her glory. But Bob remained industrious. And in the evenings, after dinner, while Newt and Deirdre went berserk in the dining room, Bob would go out and sit on deck with a beer and throw chum for sharks, as happy as an angler on Moosehead Lake.

He and J. became great allies with their shared shark fixation. One evening Bob came home with six feet of chain and an eight-inch shark hook from Harms's marina, onto which he and J. stuck one of Jerry's elite sirloins and started jigging for Jaws. Happily none was caught.

In the mornings we worked on *Xanadu*, and in the afternoons we went ashore to look for work. Eventually, I found part-time evening work bartending, and J. got a waitressing job at a Mexican restaurant, El Papagayo. She often got a ride to work with another Papagayo waitress who was living aboard a boat at Antilles boatyard in the Lagoon. One evening she came back to *Xanadu* and told me about a twenty-seven-foot-long English cutter she had seen at the boatyard. We both went to look at it the next day.

Suky, a tubby little boat hauled out of the water while its owner worked on the hull beneath a handwritten FOR SALE sign nailed to the planking, looked all wrong to me. But J. saw it—what the boat could be and us in it—before I did. I didn't like its high boxy cabin—which was painted *orange*—I thought it spoiled the boat's looks. It wasn't at all beautiful. Characterful, maybe. *Maybe.* Definitely funky inside, where it looked more like a VW bus heading out from Haight-Ashbury in 1968. It was a mongrel boat. But it had a nice long bowsprit. And it had just sailed across the Atlantic.

Its owner, a Dutchman named Henry, who wore lots of shells around his neck, told us it was a very easy boat to sail. The engine had conked out somewhere down in the Grenadines and he'd thrown it overboard and never missed it, he said. We asked why he was selling. Henry shrugged and smiled. He just wanted to try something else for a while.

What a flake, I thought, and it was a flake's boat. He was doing something with cloth and glue to the hull below the waterline and when I asked him about it he said it was this great stuff, man, Cascover sheathing, you glue it on and it keeps the worms out and you never have to caulk the hull. He was just glueing on a new patch where some of it had come loose. Henry wanted $7,000 for the boat.

We went off to work. A few more days on *Xanadu* and we began to think more about freaky *Suky*. The orange cabin could be painted white, for a start. Get Henry's junk out of there and the interior would actually much resemble the Hiscocks' *Wanderer III*. *Suky*, in fact, had much in common with the Hiscocks' boat: it had been built in 1939, eleven years before *Wanderer*; both were traditional English cruising cutters and shared many features, the main differences being *Wanderer*'s additional three feet in length, and one deeper foot in the keel which gave the Hiscocks sufficient headroom without the higher cabin top. But *Suky*'s shallower draft would enable the boat to sneak over thinner water. It would be a great boat for the shallow Bahamas, where, Eric had complained in *Atlantic Cruise in Wanderer III*, a five-and-a-half-foot draft had made them anxious, even barred them from many anchorages. *Suky* was *Wanderer*'s runty, short-legged sibling.

The boat's greatest attraction was that we thought we could scrape together enough money to buy it. We could have our own boat, which no one could sell or tell us to move off of. Our own home. Our independence.

A few days later we went back to the yard and looked at the boat again. It would certainly look better painted. Spruced up. A mongrel, yes, but you can love a mutt. It had a look that might become endearing, but at that moment it appeared forlorn and neglected with its hull exposed, unpainted, splotched with cloth and glue. And that god-awful cabin top—it was the color of sauce rouille, which looks good in bouillabaisse but not on a boat. Not on an ugly duckling that needed some help and understanding to look its best. It made me angry: Henry was clearly a philistine, a lout with no sense of boat aesthetics; a boat abuser.

He wasn't aboard. We found him at the other end of the yard, sitting at the H.M.S. Pinafore, the wreck of an old hull dragged up out of the water, chain-sawn to bartop height, a roof erected over it, now serving Heineken. We offered $5,000, subject to survey. He countered with $6,500 and the yard bill. We countered and dug in at $6,000 and the yard bill—depending on what his yard bill was. He agreed.

That night we excitedly told Newt and Deirdre and Bob about *Suky*. They were very nice about it and encouraged us. Deirdre had some old sheets she could give us. Newt said he'd survey the boat for free.

He did, a few days later. He started diligently in the bow, sticking a small screwdriver into the stem, the frames, looking for soft wood, an indication of rot. He worked aft into the bilge. Then he slowed down and stopped. He was sweating and pale, painfully hungover. He couldn't find any rot, he said, sitting down in the saloon, panting. There were a few cracked frames, which could be "sistered"—new ones built alongside the cracked ones—but nothing that needed serious attention right away. It was a small, simple boat, there were things we'd undoubtedly do to it in time, but Henry had sailed it in, so we could sail it out. His basic message was: it looks clean, what do you want for $6,000? Which was our feeling. It obviously wasn't a blue-water thoroughbred ready to punch its way around Cape Horn, but we could live on it cheaply in the Caribbean for a while and have some fun. What about that cloth all over the hull? I asked Newt. He shrugged. If it works . . .

We gave Henry $1,000 and waited for the rest to be wired from the States. All we had and some borrowed from J.'s father. Henry packed two small duffels and disappeared, and J. and I moved off *Xanadu* and aboard our new home.

Immediately, J.'s diary changes its tone again. The pages are filled with details of our days of work on the boat. On Tuesday, June 21, her birthday, she woke to a treasure hunt aboard. Still brand-new to the boat's many hidden places, this was fun for both of us, hiding and finding her presents. She got a Caribbean cookbook, and, as she had given me a year before in St. Jean aboard

Viva III, a pair of docksiders. That evening we ate fish at Daddy's, a native joint near the boatyard.

Under the amused guidance of Billy Walker, the boatyard's ship-wright (we had no idea what we were getting into, but he did), J. and I worked to get the boat back in the water. First we cleaned it, pulling years of filth out of the bilges, back into which we poured gallons of wood preservative which the holistic freaks who spent most of their time at the Pinafore bar insisted was full of Agent Orange. We replaced rusty fittings, bolts, tried to find and stop deck leaks revealed by a sudden rain, painted five-fathom marks on the anchor chain, and finally stripped the exterior of the boat of all its paint and repainted it an off-white enamel, a color named by its manufacturer "White Sand."

We discovered huge reserves of love inside us for our new boat. As it transformed almost hourly under its many coats of paint, we would step back and stare at it with profound wonder, admiration, and exactly the sort of love you'd feel for a dog you'd found abandoned in a swamp and taken home to wash off—a mutt, to be sure, but all the more lovable for its dopey imperfection. And beyond this, the thrill of knowing that we would get into this thing, with all we owned, and live in it, and start sailing around these tropical islands, and anchor for free off beaches we'd only glimpsed from ferries. We stared and stared at this little boat, and stared anew every time we left the yard and came back to it. All its bits and pieces and wood and fastenings and wire and rope and sails were ours. Never had any corporeal thing meant as much to either of us, and probably for both of us in this life, nothing ever will again.

One thing we were determined to change immediately was *that name*. Sailor's superstition has it that changing a boat's name is unlucky. However, *Suky* was not its christened original, but Henry's fond idea, and now terminally tainted by its association with him. We saw Henry now only when he came around to ask if the wired money had come through, and in response to our many questions about the boat he would tell us nothing whatsoever beyond the condescending remark, accompanied by a flaky grin, that "*Shuky's sho shimple*" that we would figure it all out ourselves. He was right, and when we did, we changed almost everything aboard the boat.

J.'s diary records the names we mulled over like expectant parents: *Papaya. Beagle* (I still like this one, partly for its nod to Darwin's and Fitzroy's doughty *Beagle*, and also because the boat, in its stocky compactness and eagerness, much resembled a nice beagle). *Magdalena. Sobrasada.* The last an indigenous Mallorquín sausage that J. loved. They're not great boat names, but most boat names are fatuous, and they had meaning for us (we liked papaya and ate a lot of it). *Magdalena* was the exception; it meant nothing to us, but for some reason that's what we started calling the boat, although we didn't yet paint that on the boat's transom stern.

The money came. Henry took it and was gone forever. Launch day arrived. The boat went into its natural element at the end of the day and we lay at anchor off the boatyard for the night. We watched the bilge fill up with water, which Billy had told us to expect after the long haul-out. It would take a night and a day, he said, for the dried-out timbers to swell up and keep the water out. We would have to pump, off and on, until then. It wasn't bad at all; a few minutes every few hours—as I'm doing now, but on that happy day it grew less and less each time.

It was almost motionless in the sheltered waters of the Lagoon, but we could feel the floating, solid stability of our new home as it heeled slightly, ponderously, when we moved about trying to orient ourselves to the new and changing views out the portholes. In the few weeks we had known the boat, it had sat up on the hard and pointed one way, the same views seen from each side. Now it turned a little this way and that around its anchor chain and the world around us slowly shifted. We lit the cozy kerosene cabin lamps. We ate on deck, marveling at the utter satellite isolation afforded by a boat even a short, swimmable distance from shore. We had left the land and were no longer dwellers upon it (and for the next five years, neither of us slept more than fifteen or twenty nights ashore). We looked across the water at landlubbers walking around the boatyard, to and from the Pinafore bar, and we pitied them. I slept fitfully, getting up often to pump and to look out a porthole to see if we had dragged anchor or were already aground. I did not yet know of the holding power of our thirty-five-pound plow anchor attached to forty fathoms of five-sixteenths-inch chain, and I was unassuaged by the windless calm. But *Magdaleña* lay still on the flat water.

At midday the next day, Billy Walker motored out in a launch to where we were anchored, threw us a line, and towed us out through the shoaling channels of the lagoon to deep water. We had cold beer and sandwiches in a cooler to share with him, but we forgot all about them in the fuss and excitement, until we had cast off his line and he was zooming back toward the mangroves and we were bobbing off the south coast of St. Thomas. On our own.

The main was already up, fluttering in the breeze, and we raised the jib and staysail, pulled in all sheets, and began tacking east. We beat toward Dog Cut, a narrow current-ripped gap between small rocky islets at the southeast tip of St. Thomas, through which we would have to sail to reach Red Hook, where we planned to spend the night. Without an engine, relying solely on our ability to work the wind and currents, I was suddenly nervous. I bolted my beer. The sandwich turned to dry mush in my mouth and I threw it over-board. I was grimly silent, concentrating on tacking the boat, and becoming disturbed by its evident sluggishness. It seemed reluctant to come about on each tack. We had bought an unhandy tub, I started thinking, almost panicking. A slow, fucking tub, and without an engine! We were probably going to smash into the rocks right here in Dog Cut before we'd gone a mile.

But then I looked at J. She was standing up on the windward side of the cockpit, face into the wind, her blond hair blowing out behind her, and she had begun to shriek. At the top of her voice she was yelling how great, how unbelievable, how beautiful it all was, and I thought she was wonderful. This was how she was heralding the start of our new life on our boat, screaming out her love of it for all she was worth. I was ashamed of my fear. She filled me with faith and I threw my crappy mood overboard and we shot through Dog Cut.

I close the diary which is red, its pages rippled and fattened with mildew, and this thing like a sneeze rises up and comes out of me and I find I am crying.

I go up into the cockpit and take a look around. No ships, empty ocean. Not much wind, but short lumpy seas from the northwest which slow *Toad* down.

I start pumping the bilge again.

July 10

Day 8—End of 1st week out of Fayal—0000: Lovely night, stars, warm. We're becalmed. Sails slatting as boat rolls sightly on imperceptible swell. Tried to go to sleep reading The Devil Drives, *life of Burton, the Victorian explorer, but riveting stuff and keeps me awake. Will try to sleep now.*

0100: Leak steady so far, pumping 2–3 minutes every 2 hours. That's better than getting worse, but it's not getting better, and conditions are light. Unnerving.

1320: Noon pos: 31°30'N, 34°08'W. 58 miles noon to noon. With the wind from calm to force 2 since yesterday noon, that's not a bad mileage. Old Toad *is moving very well in these light airs. About 500 miles from Horta in exactly one week—not as bad as it's seemed sometimes, and the fact that we're farther S than I had wanted to be may stand us in good stead later, near and beyond Bermuda, when we'll probably be forced N by SW'lies. Also, farther south may mean a gentler ride with more chance of E'lies. Present course of about 300° takes us more or less straight toward Bermuda—1,540 miles away.*

Marking the noon position—a small penciled X—on my sailing chart of the North Atlantic, I see we are now well out onto the broad belly of the ocean, the great midriff emptiness between the continental outposts of Bermuda and the Azores. 2400 fathoms (14,400 feet) down to the ocean floor. Having been pushed mostly south this last week, we're not as far east as I'd hoped to be, but in another week we should be halfway between North Africa and the east coast of the United States. On the chart, our route from one side of the Atlantic to the other looks all wrong: a long, pronounced droop from northern Europe down here to the subtropical middle of the ocean, seemingly Caribbean-bound, then back up to the northeast United States.

Certainly not the flight path of an intrepid crow, but it is the best one for *Toad*.

Planning my route across the ocean in London earlier this spring, I spread pilot charts of the North Atlantic for the months of June and July on the floor and bent over them for hours. My optimistic plan was to try to stick close to the rhumb-line—the straight-line—route from Falmouth to Fayal, to get clear of the European continent with its commercial and fishing traffic; to keep, if possible, from being blown south into the Bay of Biscay, with its notoriously rough waters, where I could expect to find myself port-hopping along the north coast of Spain against predominant westerlies. A dreary prospect, particularly as I've always thought Spain's much-ballyhooed *tapas* and *paella* are overrated dishes, usually as grease-laden and rancid as Azorean *choriço*. The June pilot chart showed mostly westerly and northwesterly winds along this route—on or just off the nose—and I had expected to be beating to windward for most of that first leg of the trip. But I was lucky. I could not have realistically hoped for the glorious easterly wind that blew gently behind us and carried us the entire 1,195 miles.

Then, planning the route from the Azores to Maine, I bent over the pilot chart for July. These pilot charts—quite different from basic sailing charts, which show only lines of longitude and latitude, water depths, and obstructions, such as rocks, shoals, or land—are the primary tool used by a navigator planning a sailing route across an ocean. Published by the Defense Mapping Agency in Washington, D.C., they show, for each month of the year, the average strength and direction of winds, currents, the percentages of calms and gales, for every 5 degrees of latitude by 5 degrees of longitude square of the ocean. They show where you might hit icebergs, the paths of tropical and extratropical cyclones, atmospheric pressure, air temperature, sea surface temperature, magnetic variation, and the routes across the ocean taken by full- and low-powered ships.

On the backs of the charts, for no other reason than to fill up that large blank space, are great freebies: illustrated articles on such subjects as: "Dangerous Sea Life" or "Satellite Navigation." You can curl up in your bunk and spend all day looking at a pilot chart.

These charts were the brainchild of Matthew Fontaine Maury, a nineteenth-century lieutenant in the U.S. Navy, who began collecting weather observations recorded in logbooks by captains aboard other ships.

Maury began this task at a time when a tremendous amount of information about remote parts of the world's oceans was becoming available for the first time. This was the heyday of the Yankee whalers, and their equally adventuresome brethren, the sealers, who were after pelts for American, European, and Chinese markets. Commerce-driven, these mariners were true explorers, pushing their slow, tubby ships beyond the limits of known frontiers as they thinned the world's oceans of its seemingly limitless resources and sailed ever farther hunting for more. It was a Nantucket sealing ship, the *Topaz*, that was the first vessel to reach Pitcairn's Island nineteen years after the *Bounty* got there in 1789, and found the last living mutineer, Alexander Smith. An American whaler, the *Manhattan,* of Sag Harbor, cruised the Japan "grounds" and anchored off what is now Tokyo eight years before U.S. Commodore Perry historically "opened up" Japan in 1853. And it was whalers following bowhead whales into high arctic latitudes that brought back volumes of grim descriptions of the conditions there.

Millions of observations later, Maury's charts give the sailor a full statistical picture of conditions most likely to be encountered in every part of every ocean, in every month of the year. But weather out at sea is no more predictable than ashore, and on any given day—as for the entire twelve days of my passage from Falmouth to Horta—the pilot charts can be wrong.

The navigator, heading out onto the featureless deep, places a religious faith in his books, charts, sextant, timepiece, and leadline.

These tools acquire talismanic importance. When they fail or mislead him he is unreasonably upset.

In 1968, racing west-about around the world, singlehanded, nonstop, Englishman Robin Knox-Johnston was confronted with days and weeks of steady easterlies down in the Southern Ocean, in the latitudes of the "Roaring Forties," where, according to the pilot charts and centuries of sailors' lore, strong westerlies are supposed to prevail. At the time, his most serious competitor, Frenchman Bernard Moitessier, who had left Europe weeks after Knox-Johnston, was 4,000 miles astern. It wasn't far enough, given Moitessier's larger boat, greater speed, and the certainty that, of course, the Frenchman would be getting what the pilot charts predicted. The contrary weather, against all his expectations, drove Knox-Johnston to his greatest heights of frustration and brought out his best English schoolboy xenophobia:

> December 9th, 1968 . . . Of all the lousy things to happen; easterlies in an area which is renowned for westerlies. . . . If the Frogs are meant to win—OK, but there is no need to torture me as well as allowing me to lose, and the Chinese could hardly have thought up a slower, more destructive method of torturing a person than this. . . .

> December 10th, 1968. No change still. I cannot make it out at all. . . . Perhaps if I decided to turn round and head back to New Zealand I'd get westerlies! . . .

> December 29th, 1968 . . . I just give up! Someone is going to have to rewrite the books! . . .

> December 30th, 1968 . . . Tacking north and south and making no progress at all, whilst somewhere to the west and probably not far away now, I'll bet the Frenchman is having beautiful westerlies.

Planning *Toad*'s route back in England, I decided to try to follow, more or less, the dotted line on my June and July pilot charts marking the route of low-powered vessels westbound from northern Europe to New York. This is an old steamer route, probably little used nowadays, with ships heading more directly for their destinations, but it takes advantage of winds and currents, and *Toad* certainly qualifies as a low-powered vessel. This line heads southwest from the English Channel, through the Azores, to a dot on the chart at $33°00'$ north, $38°33'$ west—about 1,300 miles due west of Morocco. Along this course, beyond the Azores, the pilot chart shows winds coming mostly from the northeast and east, and ocean currents of about half a knot pushing me in the right direction. This dot is almost 600 miles from Fayal. From there, the line heads due west 1,200 miles to another dot just north of Bermuda, at $33°00'$ north, $65°00'$ west. Between these dots, the wind is supposed to shift gradually from easterly to southwesterly, with the current still in my favor. (This line also passes *north* of the location of an iceberg sighted in July 1916, the chart notes, 500 miles south of the *mean* maximum southerly limit for icebergs in July. I could pause at this detail and wonder what sort of year it's been for ice up north, but I let it go. I can't believe I could pump this much to keep *Toad* afloat and then run into an iceberg here at the edge of the tropics.) At this point—the Bermuda dot, I call it—I will turn half-right and head for Maine, 800 miles distant, with an increased likelihood of southwesterlies, which will then be on or just abaft our beam, fair sailing. Inevitably, I will be blown off this line, one side or the other, but it offers what is statistically the most advantageous course to follow, and I will try to keep to it.

The blue "wind roses"—circles with feathered arrows indicating wind directions and strengths, centered on each 5-degree square on a pilot chart—also indicate that this course promises light winds, an average of force 3 (seven to ten knots), and calms about 6 percent of the time. These are the "Horse Latitudes," a place of notoriously light winds between the trade winds to the south and the stronger westerlies to the north, an area of ocean where progress can seem painfully slow. In the age of sail, merchant ships often took months to get through the Horse Latitudes, by which time the seamen had worked off what they called the "dead horse," the advance wages they had received when signing on. A slow passage here was to a seaman's benefit, as he was paid by the day, and a slow start meant a longer passage; thus to "flog a dead horse" was vainly to expect an energetic effort from seamen as they worked off their advance.

Light winds will mean a slow trip, but a gentle one, and especially now with *Toad*'s leak this is what I want. A slow poke across the Atlantic, no challenges, no rough stuff. I have plenty of food, books, batteries for the radio, and I'm already home, so speed doesn't particularly concern me.

Tonight, at sunset, listening to jazz on VOA, I make a pie: Dried apricots and apple rings from Neal's Yard, raisins, a bit of trail mix, my bread dough without yeast. It's delicious and I'm amazed it turns out so well, like a real pie. That I can do this with my funky ingredients. I have it with a little tinned cream poured over the top. A Sunday treat. After that I pump out the water seeping into the bilge. Pumping has become a part of my routine, and sometimes, like tonight, listening to jazz and thinking about my pie and what else I might bake, I can do it without growing appalled at how long it takes until I hear the loud suck of air beneath the floorboards.

July 12

After several days of very light northeasterlies, this morning the wind veers into the northwest and confuses me. I believe we are on the southeastern edge of the Azores High, a great isobaric mesa that stretches at this time of year between the Azores and Bermuda. With winds blowing clockwise around any high-pressure system, northeasterlies would place us at the southeast—or at the four or five o'clock position—of this clockwise system.

So why northwesterlies—which would indicate a one or two o'clock position—now? Why doesn't it work the way it's supposed to, according to the basic principles of weather systems, according to Maury's charts, according to the time-honored lore handed down by all those salty seafarers who have gone this way before? Why are there always so many exceptions to the supposed rules that the rules themselves, as Knox-Johnston complained, seem in need of revision? I can only presume it's just a small anomalous wobble in the high.

Sometimes I think I would like to have a weatherfax machine. In that next boat. Ships have them, and the big yachts with bucks. You get a faxed printout from any number of sophisticated weather stations ashore every time you press a button. A weather map of your area, dense with isobars and wind roses, explanations and forecasts written in stone. So you don't do what I do: sit in the cockpit, look up into the sky, and wonder what the fuck is going on.

But if I had a weatherfax machine, I'd have to throw away my weather rhymes:

> *When the wind shifts against the sun*
> *Trust it not, for back it will run.*

This morning the wind *veered:* it moved from northeast to northwest, or in the direction of the sun's passage. But had it *backed,* moved contrary to the sun—say, from northwest to northeast, or southwest to south or southwest—then I might have thought of this rhyme, not trusted this wind shift, and waited for it to shift back again. As it is, the wind might sit in the northwest indefinitely now, forcing us to beat.

On the other hand, it did happen quite quickly:

> *Long foretold, long last*
> *Short warning, soon past.*

Sailors found these rhymes accurate, put their faith in them, and passed them on. Some, apparently so unerringly useful, have been purloined by landlubbers ashore:

> *Red sky at night is a sailor's [or shepherd's] delight;*
> *Red sky in the morning, the sailor takes warning.*

Many times a day—each time I make an entry on the left-hand page of my daily log—I look at the barometer. Its reading will considerably affect my own inner barometer:

> *At sea with low and falling glass,*
> *Soundly sleeps the careless ass.*
> *But when the glass is high and rising*
> *Soundly sleeps the careful wise one.*

But it must already be *high and rising,* because there's a rhyme that warns me to look out for a sudden rise after a low:

> *Quick rise after low*
> *Foretells a stronger blow.*

There are many such rhymes, about the appearance of the sky, when and how the wind blows, handed down from sailor to sailor as long as old salts have broken in new ones:

> Mackerel sky and mares' tails
> Make lofty ships carry low sails.
>
> . . .
>
> If rain before wind, tops'l sheets and halyards mind.
> If wind before rain, soon you may make sail again.
>
> . . .
>
> When clouds appear like rocks and towers,
> The earth's refreshed by frequent showers.
>
> . . .
>
> When the sea-hog jumps,
> Look out for your pumps.

This last refers to the debatable lore that porpoises leaping close inshore may augur stormy weather. True or not, I like it, and if I see dolphins or porpoises leaping close to shore, this old saw comes to mind.

More than their possible usefulness, what I like about these rhymes is the company they bring me. They give me a kinship with sailors of the past, common seamen, as frightened as I by the prospect of hard weather, who looked skyward and mumbled to themselves:

> If clouds appear as if scratched by a hen,
> Get ready to reef your topsails then.

And then looked aft, anxiously, to the officers strutting on the poop deck, awaiting the order to run up the shrouds and get those bloody topsails in. They were superstitious men, largely ignorant of the science and theories that lay behind the phenomena they observed at sea. For them the natural world was riven with magic and mystery, examples of which might appear at any moment, between a wave, inside a cloud. They saw, as I have seen, the sun flash green on sinking into the ocean, the heavens hung with glowing curtains, and pellets of fire in the water around a ship's hull at night. Books have explained these strange sights to me, stripped them of their wonder with cold science, but the sailors of old remained ignorant and felt their magic.

If I had a weatherfax machine, the mystery and surprise of what will happen next upon the ocean and in the sky would be removed, and too much else would be taken away with the not knowing.

At 1335 I take the local noon shot and work out our position. 31°30' north, 37°31' west. I plot this on the chart and measure the distance from yesterday's fix. In the lightest of winds, we've sailed 88 miles since yesterday at local noon, which is better than I'd have imagined. About 1,900 miles to the USA.

July 14

Twelve days from Horta.

At noon today, looking down at my chart—a view from outer space if the paper were the ocean it represents—we appear to be about halfway across. Not necessarily in time or distance sailed, but visually: we appear to be halfway between North Africa and, say, the Carolinas.

More water may be leaking in. I spend nearer to three minutes pumping every few hours. However, I seem to be avoiding any effort to gauge the rate. I haven't noted in the log the frequency of my pumping, which I imagine a really tough, hard-core single-hander with the courage to face anything the ocean might throw at him would do. At night, particularly, I manage to put it out of my mind by pumping desultorily when I come up half asleep for a lookout. I don't really want to know about the whole thing.

But I'm convinced now that *Toad* remains structurally sound, that the problem is Henry's goddamn Cascover sheathing, even if, in my brief snorkel overboard, I didn't see it delaminating anywhere. I think the water's seeping under it, somehow, and coming in through planking seams and joints wherever the old caulking has dried out and shrunk. And there's nothing I can do about it. A hole in the bow I might be able to patch, but a thin leaking scrim spread over the entire hull can only be repaired by hauling out and ripping the sheathing all off and caulking the seams anew. All I can do is keep on pumping and get there.

Shortly before midnight, roused by my bleating alarm clock, I stick my head up into the cockpit and see a ship's lights.

2340: Tried calling a ship passing a few miles N. No answer. I'm watching it for a minute or so to make sure we pass in the night with good clearance. We're becalmed, sails slatting, though zephyrs are NE'ly, which would be nice a little stronger.

Project Arabia is the ship—they just called back—and had a nice chat with the Kraut O.O.W. (Officer on Watch). Container ship. They're headed for Baltimore, then back to the Med. Nice to talk with someone. He says I make a pretty poor radar picture. I'll probably hoist a plastic bag full of aluminum foil up the mast when I get to foggy Maine.

First ship I've seen for a while. First time I've spoken with anyone since leaving the Azores. I don't expect them down here, far south of the high-powered shipping lanes, and most ships are high-powered now. But it's a comfort. There are others abroad in the world.

In the dark I can't see *Project Arabia*'s shape, only its lights, port red and white bow and stern, the lights of any ship at night. In the dark I can imagine that it looks the way I want it to look: a much older vessel, a tramp steamer, with plumb bow, raking masts and funnel; a ship Conrad's Marlow would have seen going down the sea reach of the Thames estuary in the long English twilight while he sat Buddha-like against the mizzenmast of the tide-rode yawl *Nellie* telling his friends about the horror-turned Kurtz.

It would also be one of Mr. East's ships.

I came by a love of ships and much of the romance I feel for the sea not by being dandled on the knee of a hoary sea-captain great-grandfather stinking of rum and linseed oil, or by having a keen boating dad, for none of these was available. I was taught about ships at school, by Mr. East.

In the 1950s, when we still lived in Connecticut, my mother's father and mother made a number of trips to Europe. For several of these they embarked by ship, and we—spruced up, slicked down—went into New York to see them off. This was all I knew of New York in those early days: a ride through the skyscraper canyons to the Cunard Line pier on the west side. There I got a glimpse of travel at its grandest before such a world disappeared: men in cashmere coats, women in furs, everyone well hatted; stevedores moving great mounds of matching bespoke luggage; uniformed Cunard officers welcoming passengers aboard as if they were royalty. We traipsed through the *Queen Mary*'s first-class dining halls, lounges, staterooms, all of it huge, sumptuous, grand, densely upholstered, set off by gilt and hardwood, inlaid veneers, extravagant murals. You can only see it now in books (although the *Queen Mary* is rotting at her tourist berth in Long Beach, California; but I don't think I could go aboard).

This, apparently, was travel.

Pretty soon we were pulled off, down the gangplank, and the ship—an impossibly big art deco building, looking immense even alongside Manhattan—moved away from the dock with such solid deliberation that it felt as if the dock were moving backward instead. Out into the Hudson River, pulled by tiny tugs, the ship turned for one lovely profile view, when the whole of it could be grasped, and then it slid from sight.

But I don't think I got any romance of the sea from that. I didn't see the sea, just a scrap of the Hudson, and New Jersey on the other side. They were going across the ocean to Europe. So what? I wanted to go home and play with my Fanner Fifty and watch *Gunsmoke*.

Then, in 1959, my parents decided that we were going to start a new life and move to England where my father would "sell space"—it was many years before I understood this meant selling space in magazine pages to advertisers, and I had a rather billowy, amorphous impression of how my father made his living. And more years, until after the failure of *Viva III* and my parents' divorce, until I saw this move in a less whimsical context. But at the time, when I was nine years old, it seemed like a neat idea. Something along the lines of what my grandparents did, only for longer. Again we drove to the Cunard Line pier, this time boarding the Cunarder *Caronia*. Five days at sea, of which I remember little except closing my brother's head in the elevator doors—by accident, I swore to my mother—and seeing *Some Like It Hot* four times in one day in the ship's free theater. No romance of the sea. Movies, yes.

My parents had told my brother, sister, and me that in England they spoke English, as we did. But as the *Caronia* drew alongside the dock in Southampton, up over the rail came a whiff of the separation I would come to know in the years ahead, brought about by the sharing of that common tongue:

"Come on 'en! Bungit over 'eeah! 'Ang abaht! Mind yer noggin, mate! Blimey! 'Eeah, wos yor gime? Gettat bleedin' fingmebob aht the way! 'Ass it! Bob's yer uncle!"

A tiny car was waiting for us dockside. My parents strapped trunks to its roof, drew a circle on a map around London, and we drove off into the English countryside to look for a new home.

This was England fourteen years after the end of World War II, and it looked to me then as strange and foreign as it would look to a nine-year-old English boy today. I remember seeing at close range through the car window, as we lumbered along a narrow lane in the Kentish Weald, my father getting used to the car's gears, an over-taking motorcycle-and-sidecar. Never seen one of those before. The man at the handlebars wore goggles, tweed cap, mackintosh, well-shined shoes. In the sidecar sat his wife, in scarf, goggles, and mackintosh, and strapped onto the sidecar behind her was a dead, unplucked chicken. Few English children today have seen unwrapped meat on the carcass of its original owner impaled for view in the window of the High Street butcher's shop. Today's England with its generic supermarkets is much more like the United States, and I would have recognized it instantly in 1959.

We landed, eventually, in Sevenoaks, in Kent, about 25 miles south of London. We children were dropped immediately into local schools. I went to Bayham Road Primary School, for boys, a small pebble-and-brick Victorian house with some later unattractive prefab structures, partly painted a hopeful Scandinavian orange, pressed up against it. Mr. Hill was the headmaster, and he was fond of giving the boys encouraging "talks" in the gym on Monday mornings. One of these I remember, I believe verbatim, from that distant time:

"Look down. Go on. What do you see down there on the floor? Feet. Among the many, two of them are yours. I shouldn't imagine you chaps think of your feet very often, do you? Why bother? There they are, down there, getting on with their job, and up top you're getting on with yours. Just feet, eh? But you know, it's the old feet that get you where you're going, day after day, year after year. And uncomplainingly for the most part."

Everywhere in the gym, we boys began to look at our feet, at our neighbors' feet. Now that you looked at them, they did seem to be a rum extremity. No four alike. Up at the front of the gym, on both sides of Mr. Hill, teachers—"masters," they were called— were trying desperately not to look at their own feet.

"But ignore them too long and your feet'll let you know all about it! Athlete's foot! Verucas! Bunions! Ingrowing toenails! Suddenly you're hobbled, can't go anywhere! The old feet have gone on strike! And then see where you are. Stuck, a prisoner, sitting on your backside, probably developing a good case of piles. So spare a thought for the old feet. Give them a jolly good scrubbing when you take your bath. Dry them carefully, especially between the toes. And trim the nails—but not too short!"

Such was my earliest instruction at school in England. Well beyond the scope of anything I had been learning back in the States.

I was in Mr. East's class—or form, as it was called. I have to presume we had lessons in English, math, history, and so on, but I remember nothing of that. I remember only studying ships to the exacting requirements of Mr. East. We looked at books of ships. He drew ships and their complete deck plans on the blackboard. He took us on outings up to London, to Tilbury and West India Docks and the Isle of Dogs, where we gazed at the creamy-hulled P&O liners and the lavender-hulled Union Castle liners, while Mr. East pointed out the decks and the arrangement of the superstructure, just as we had learned at school from his diagrams. He took us aboard these ships and explained the workings of the lifeboat falls, the windlasses, and we ran our little hands over the giant links of anchor chain.

"Cor! Crikey! Crumbs!" we all said.

He took us to the merchant docks, where cargo ships were unloading rum, sugar, and tropical hardwoods that prickled the insides of our noses. He pointed out the derricks and explained the meaning of the truncated sections of superstructure, so different from the long, uninterrupted promenade decks on the liners. On the bus returning to Sevenoaks we drank a terrible English soda pop called Tizer, and ate gobstoppers and sherbert lollies.

Back in school Mr. East read us the poetry of John Masefield. He made us memorize the third verse of *Cargoes*, and we sat in class chanting it like a mantra:

> *Dirty British Coaster with a salt-caked smoke stack,*
> *Butting through the Channel in the mad March Days,*
> *With a cargo of Tyne Coal,*
> *Road-rails, pig-lead,*
> *Firewood, iron-ware, and cheap tin trays.*

We shouted it!

He told us how the Orient Line's *Orion*, built for the Australian run, was launched by wireless when His Royal Highness the Duke of Gloucester pressed a button in Brisbane, Australia, and the ship rolled down the ways at Barrow-in-Furness, Lancashire.

"Cor!" we breathed, amazed at the power of science.

What I remember most of Mr. East's class is making models of ships. We made them out of balsa wood: thick pieces for the hulls, thin sections, painstaking layer upon layer, for the super-structures. We made liners and cargo ships, but I think it was the cargo ships, Masefield's rust- and salt-streaked British coaster, and the once-ubiquitous, now entirely vanished tramp steamers that were closest to Mr. East's heart. He explained them to us meticulously, their workings, the colors of their shipping lines that we painted on our model funnels, where they went (invariably to some outpost of the British Empire colored Empire pink in our inky atlases), and what they carried in their holds.

He was rigorous in his standards for our model-making. Our little hulls had plenty of curve and sheer to them, achieved not by hacking at them with our model knives, but by the steady, tiresome application of sandpaper of increasingly fine grits. Then, once the shape of a hull was approved—brought up for Mr. East's inspection at the front of the room—we sanded it fair and smooth. This fairing of the compound curves of the hull was, as it is in real-life wooden boatbuilding, a difficult task, particularly with the fibrous and hairy balsa wood. Mr. East instructed us to gauge the smoothness of our hulls by rubbing them across the skin between our noses and our upper lips. This was the most sensitive area of skin on our bodies, he told the class of nine-year-old boys, and the skin above our lips was sure to pick up the imperfections in our ships' hulls. We sat there rubbing our model ship hulls across our faces.

What class was this? Because this wasn't a onetime thing. This was what I did at Bayham Road School. Any other area of the curriculum I have forgotten. I recall a vague snapshot from a geography book: a photograph of a ship loading cargo in some East African port. I'm sure if any of Mr. East's pupils had gone on to join the merchant navy, they would have immediately shot to the top of the class.

Did we have fun doing this? Surely we enjoyed the outings to see ships, but the model-making probably took on some of the drudgery of any school endeavor: this was day-in, day-out stuff. I stopped building ships the moment I left Bayham Road. It never turned into a hobby at home. Where are those models now? I took them home, but I must have thrown them out to make room for comic books, bowie knives, and Beatle albums. They were, after all, only junk from school.

I wish I'd kept just one.

And who was Mr. East? Did he ache to be on a rusty British tramp heading up the great, gray, green, greasy Limpopo River with a cargo of firewood, ironware, and cheap tin trays? Or was he simply an "enthusiast," as the English say, like a trainspotter, or a birder, or a philatelist? He was tall and thin, beaky-nosed, wore glasses, and dressed well in that negligent British way, with rather good brown shoes—or this is what I think I remember. I can see him in P&O officer whites on the bridge of a good ship, but not in overalls shoveling coal on his way up through the ranks. I imagine he was bookish, well-read-up on far-flung places, probably rather pained about Britain's shriveling position in the world; a keen rambler, who possibly also had an appreciation for fine locomotives. But I don't know. Was there a Mrs. East? Again, I don't know, but I think not. He seems, in my memory, to be the exemplary bachelor, a man living a life taken up with his own interests.

So at the age of nine, without wanting it or thinking about it, I absorbed from the passion of Mr. East, and through the prepubescent skin above my upper lip, a sense of the beauty of ships.

I only spent three months, the fall term of 1959, at Bayham Road. My parents had discovered it wasn't a very good school. Some of the boys—like my friend Dave Gilbertson, who wore a grimy double-breasted gray flannel suit from the Co-op that I coveted—were working-class yobbos. I would realize this later on. My sister and I were already taking riding lessons on Sundays, dressed in jodhpur boots and Harris tweed hacking jackets. We had to go to the right schools. That's part of what being in England was all about.

Mr. East seemed genuinely sorry when he learned I was leaving. Perhaps he liked my ships. Perhaps, though I wouldn't remember, I showed a promising skill at shipbuilding. But one day when Dave Gilbertson and I had done some naughty anarchic thing and were scarpering off to the bog, and I was shouting, in the low accent I adopted at school, "Look out, Dave, the bloody prefects are coming!" we ran into Mr. East around a corner and he literally collared us. He looked at us with disgust. And to me he said: "I'm glad you're leaving." And I was cut to the quick.

But I think he would be pleased to know that one of his boys didn't become an insurance sales rep or a grocer or fruiterer, but went off to sea in his own little boat when he grew up, and was forever mad about ships, and when their lights passed him in the night, he thought of Mr. East.

July 15

0145: Becalmed.

0900: Still becalmed.

1000: Saw a bottle and thought I could see a note in it. Much excitement. Drifted over to it, but it was empty. Thought of the bottles J. used to put messages in and throw overboard. Would like to find one of those now.

1130: Have found U.S. Mutual news on shortwave. Temperature in the 80s and thunderstorms in New England today. Zephyrs from SW out here.

1350: Noon pos: 31°15'N, 41°29'W. 35 miles noon to noon. Depressing.

Today the leak is clearly worse, and I've done the manly thing and gotten some education. I pumped fifty strokes per minute, five full minutes, two and a half hours after the last pump-out. That's easily about double what it was a week ago. The pump is a Whale Gusher, model number 15. I presume this means it pumps out fifteen gallons per minute. Seventy-five gallons I pumped out.

Is that a lot? I don't know what to compare it to. It's not too frightening as long as I can pump it out. It's a little less than *Toad's* total freshwater capacity of around ninety gallons, held in two trapezoidal-sectioned, six-foot-long tanks beneath the saloon bunks. That's a lot of water.

But not enough to sink the boat—yet. Not enough even to come above the floorboards—I usually start pumping when I feel I may soon see salt water washing over the floorboards because I know I would find this a disturbing sight.

It doesn't even take up a lot of time. What's five minutes every few hours?

But if it's double what it was a week ago, there is a time factor here. I can pump it out of sight and mind now, but it's getting worse, faster. The leak and I are in a race to dry land.

We've been sailing over a millpond. What is going to happen, I wonder, when the wind picks up, as I've been wishing it would, and as it certainly will do eventually?

2000: Great salad for dinner, but, alas, the end of my fruit & veg—though I have some onions, potatoes, and a bit of rubbery cabbage.

2200: Becalmed.

2300: A breeze coming across the glassy sea. I feel it on my skin, then it rustles the sails, fills them into pale parabolic kites, and we begin to move. The water gurgles astern in a new wake.

July 16

1335: Noon pos: 31°34'N, 42°47'W. An astounding 69 miles noon to noon. How did we manage that becalmed most of the day yesterday? Must be some help from current there. And a great morale boost: I'm now on the western half of my N. Atlantic chart. Both Maine and today's position are in view as it lies on the chart table.

1945: Becalmed. I feel I'll never get away from here.

2300: A breeze again, same as this time last night. We're moving and it's wonderful.

July 17

In the late afternoon I pass another doughty voyager: a *Physalia*, or Portuguese man-of-war. It's headed in the opposite direction, east, toward Europe. To Portugal? Its "sail," a translucent half-round gas-filled chamber about six inches long and almost as high above the water—about the size and shape of a large clamshell—and the same lovely pale lavender color as the old Union Castle liners, has enough parabolic curve to enable it to sail to windward. This is the sort of weather it likes best, a flat sea, the lightest of breezes, sailing at a gentle angle of heel. In stronger winds it gets blown flat, but this is an efficient form of reefing, as the wind spills off its sail and it effectively lies ahull until the blow is over, its underwater feeding streamers providing better drag for volume than the deepest keel of any yacht, and not too much hard-won sea room is lost.

Farther on, I see another one. Then several more. A colony, or a family. Perhaps a race.

There is much of the Portuguese man-of-war about *Toad*. A design evolved not for speed, but for a dogged ability to get there in the end, and, in the meantime, to be at home upon the ocean. Yet even after six years of living aboard, I have been astonished by *Toad*'s performance in the calm or nearly windless conditions of this last week. Every day the noon-to-noon run has exceeded all my expectations. In the lightest of airs, *Toad* has moved and kept moving longer, farther, faster than I thought was possible for its shape, which, underwater, where it counts, is scientifically crude.

Part of the reason I'm so surprised is that I, like everyone else, am a victim of received opinion, of conventional thinking, of the wisdom of the books. *Toad*, according to the books, is all wrong. Its hull below the waterline is fat and bulbous, rather like the belly of an elephant between its legs. It lacks the finer-angled bow and stern of shapelier, more hydrodynamically thoughtful yachts, which shoulder the water aside in gradual increments and pull it back into the wake with a minimum of turbulent displacement. *Toad* is shaped more like a half-submerged gypsy caravan, full in the ends, so that it has to work harder pushing water aside.

Toad's keel, a long, untrimmed balk of lumber, lacks any hint of a foil shape   the sectional shape of an airplane's wing: rounded at the front, reaching its greatest width about a third the way back, then tapering to a fine point at its end. A boat's keel should be so shaped for the same reason: to part the water with as little turbulence as possible, and draw it back together smoothly. Tank tests have provided the optimum shapes. Most modern yachts have fin keels: deep, narrow foil shapes, like wings pointing straight down into the deep.

According to all the books, *Toad* should be barely able to move out of its own way. A monstrously inefficient design. A tub. In this it stands with some notable company: "Probably no vessel was less suited for long-distance cruising than Slocum's *Spray*," writes sailor-designer Skip Dashew. The *Spray* was an engineless oyster dredger with a hull design about three hundred years old, rebuilt by Slocum and then sailed around the world by him alone between 1895 and 1898. Critics have for years insisted that Slocum's claims for its exemplary behavior at sea must have been exaggerated. However, a number of people have built *Spray* replicas and fervently defend Slocum and reiterate his claims. Dashew goes on: "I doubt if Robin Knox-Johnston would have sailed a Swahili [*sic*] if he could have afforded a more modern design."*

This is quite true: Knox-Johnston tried to get sponsorship to build a faster, more modern design in which to circumnavigate. He failed to get the money and went finally in *Suhaili* because it was his own boat, all he had. The clunkiest, oldest, most "inefficient" design

---

*Knox-Johnston's boat was called *Suhaili*, and it was built for him in India, but Dashew, who spent some time in South Africa, has trolled his memory or sources too casually.

of the nine boats that set out to race around the world in 1968, it was also the only boat to finish.

The question of "efficiency" in yacht design rages on ad infinitum between sailors and yacht designers, and it's endlessly silly. *Efficiency* has been confused with speed and performance. Modern yachts are without question faster than older boats, and able to point closer to the wind when tacking. But you wouldn't want a race car to go to the Safeway on Saturday mornings loaded with the kids and a dog. It wouldn't be an efficient design. And you wouldn't want a lightweight, pointy, rule-distorted weekend racer to load with provisions and sail around the world.

So radically has yacht design changed in the last thirty years that many people today are surprised that older designs can even move through the water. The *Westsail 32*, a mass-produced fiberglass boat based on a very old design, is said to be an unhandy tub, a poor sailer, unable to tack without the engine going to push its nose through the eye of the wind. A yacht designer of some tiny note who had never sailed one repeated this nonsense to me once. It is fat and tubby, like *Toad*, roomy inside and sea-kindly in motion. It was drawn in 1924 by William Atkin for *Motor Boat* magazine, as a design that the magazine's readers might have knocked together for them by local boatbuilders for a modest sum. Atkin called his little boat *Eric*—after the Red—and based the design on a Norwegian lifeboat craft known as a *redningskoite*, which was in turn based on the ancient seaworthy double-enders used by Scandinavian fisher-men venturing into the North Sea as far as the Lofoten Islands north of the Arctic Circle; and those boats were essentially short, fat versions of the Viking longships of a thousand years ago. In the 1970s, Westsail's designer Bill Crealock redrew Atkin's *Eric* for fiberglass construction at the same moment that sailors everywhere suddenly tired of flimsy daysailer designs strengthened for cruising; they wanted a massively strong, purpose-built boat, capable of going anywhere. The little Americanized *redningskoite* became the VW Bug of the yachting world. Westsail was for a time the success story of Southern California boatbuilders. By the late seventies, eight hundred had been built, and *Time* magazine had done a cover story on the popularity of small-boat cruising, featuring Westsail and its tubby prototype. But by the eighties, Westsail had gone bankrupt and its boat had fallen from grace. Such a fat long-keeler (as opposed to a modern design with a short, deep fin keel) surely could not sail well, people said, looking up from their yachting monthlies, and the mob turned again toward faster, lighter, newer boats.

Robin Knox-Johnston's supposed dog of a "Swahili," *Suhaili*, is an Atkin *Eric*, a sister ship to the *Westsail 32*. Since returning to fame and glory in 1969 after his record circumnavigation, he has gone on to other sailing feats: he has raced across the Atlantic and around the world on trimarans and catamarans of record-breaking speed. He knows all about efficiency under sail. However, it was *Suhaili* he chose to sail to Greenland, above the Arctic Circle, on a recent climbing-sailing expedition with British mountaineer Chris Bonington and four other men. The choice of ship in which to sail to such a place is not made by nostalgia.

I know, then, that such fat, tubby boats, can in fact sail well, that they are good sea boats. But what amazes me now, in the ghosting conditions of this last week, is how well *Toad* has performed in such light conditions. Its momentum has kept it going through almost breathless air.

I have always felt sensitive to the notion that *Toad* is a slow, unhandy tub. This is what people would think, looking at it and knowing what the books say—this is even what *I* thought. But what do they know of this boat in its element? Has it not, as my brother David shouted, been to more places than the snide publican of Flushing has had hot dinners? Certainly it has traveled farther, with less fuss, then most of the plastic clone wonderboats that sit unused in all the marinas of the world.

I have always seen *Toad* as the interim boat, the boat I would poke around in on both sides of the Atlantic before selling and getting "the right one," that faster, bigger, sleeker thoroughbred that I would sail to Rarotonga, Whangaroa, and over horizons beyond. But now, deep into this fine voyage, that sense of another boat being better has dissolved. I think I have felt for some time, since Horta if not before, that I cannot sell *Toad*. I'll get some job and buy J. out of her share. For as surely as the Portuguese man-of-war can sail across the Atlantic, *Toad* can take me around the world, and handsomely. It's the best boat a boy ever had.

It's just got this leak. If I can get it to Maine, I'll pull the sheathing off and recaulk the hull properly. It will be better than new. Then paint it a beautiful off-white and go.

July 20

0900: Becalmed.

1730: I've been hearing whatever it is again. Standing on the cabin roof beside the mast, the sea oily smooth over a vestigial swell, I can hear something. Actually, I'm not sure I hear it at all. I've become aware of it over the last few days during such absolute calms when the boat is quite still, when there's no sound of water along the hull, no sound of waves. It's a rumbling, possibly below the level of what I would call sound. I think it may be the heaving of the ocean upon the earth's crust, this ocean that is pulled back and forth by the moon, and rises and falls by the pressure of the earth's atmosphere upon it. An oceanic inhaling and exhaling. Or maybe thermocline layers of icy water moving across slopes or obstructions on the ocean floor 18,000 feet below me. Maybe it's tinnitus, something in my inner ear—a version of "the sea" one hears in sea shells cupped to the ear. But I can hear it.

Tonight, at twilight, a breeze comes across the water, as it has the last few evenings, and I start fiddling with the sails to make the most of it. *Toad* begins to glide off from a standstill, and as always I feel a thrill at the sensation of being suddenly lifted and borne away under sail.

I believe you can learn enough about sailing technique in one morning to set off on a voyage around the world that afternoon. I don't mean seamanship—the experience-honed judgment needed to handle a boat in all situations, which is the greatest requirement of the sailor—I mean the simple basic principles of how to move a boat with sails for any given wind. These principles are as follows: If the wind is from ahead, you pull the sails in; if the wind is from the side, you let them out a bit; if it's from behind, you let the sails way out. That's it. That'll get you out of the harbor; in fact, if you have an engine, you'll probably motor out of the harbor and put your sails up later. That's what most people do. The finer points of sail trim take years to learn, years of pulling the sails in and out until the wind is no longer invisible but is something you can see as clearly as smoke, with all its wraiths and streamers and eddies as its moves over the surface of the sea and slipstreams through your rigging and around your mast and across the parabolas of your sails. By then you know where the wind is with your eyes shut, you can feel it in your sleep in your bunk below, and a small change can wake you up. Trimming your sails then to make the most of the wind becomes an instinct. But in the beginning, pulling sails in when the wind is ahead, letting them out when the wind is behind, will take you far. Especially if you begin doing this on a boat with an engine which you can flip on when the wind grows light or fickle or when you want to sail through a tight spot. Early on, you may think you know how to sail. That's what I thought before J. and I began sailing aboard *Magdaleña*.

Our first voyage was back to Tortola, where we had been happy. We were cruising sailors now, aboard our own boat, and we wouldn't have any problems with the immigration authorities. Since *Magdaleña* was so much smaller than *Viva III*, I had imagined it would be nimbler, more responsive than my parents' boat. But it seemed less so; it moved sluggishly to windward—as it had on our first passage from the Lagoon—and it took us an entire afternoon (according to J.'s second-year diary, which I am dipping into tonight) to tack the three miles across Pillsbury Sound from Red Hook to Caneel Bay on St. John. Again, I worried that we'd bought a dog. If we had been aboard *Viva* I would certainly have turned on the engine and steamed straight across out of frustration, and it occurred to me that since I had always had that option, and too often used it, my sailing skills were probably still quite elementary.

At anchor that evening, I opened Eric Hiscock's *Cruising Under Sail*:

The usual fault the beginner makes when sailing close-hauled is to sheet his sails in too flat and then to point up too close to the wind, so that although his yacht may head in the desired direction she does not move fast enough through the water. The average cruising yacht [that is, of the period in which Hiscock was writing] when treated in this manner will become lifeless and drift away to leeward; her sheets should be eased a little to get her moving. . . . This is also known as sailing . . . "full-and-by."

That is, keeping the sails full and sailing by the wind, rather than by directional desire.

We tried this "full-and-by" business the next day and we did better. In time we also learned, per Hiscock, to sail the boat around from one tack to the other, rather than jamming the tiller hard over and trying to come about as fast as a modern boat. And we learned to "back" a headsail: to let it fill with wind on the windward side of the new tack before releasing its sheet; this helped push the boat's nose around. We learned to look at the "cat's-paws" and small wavelets made by the wind on the water to see where the *true* wind rather than the *apparent* wind (which is the wind plus the air coming from the bow made by the boat's forward movement) was coming from. These simple lessons were the key to handling this fat little engineless boat, but they were not learned at once. Tacking into West End, Tortola, months later, we pinched too close to windward, failed to come about, and the bowsprit drove straight through a bush ashore, stopping a foot from an old man walking along the road beside the water. He said: "You got to turn de boat before you get dis close."

In Tortola, we saw Mike Underhill and his kids Sally and Ian and they came aboard and admired the boat. We hitched around the island as we'd done before and we loved it again, but now that we had our boat, the act of pulling up the anchor and going somewhere else was so exciting that we knew immediately we wouldn't stay long. On the Fourth of July, four people asked us to sail them to Cruz Bay on St. John for $5 apiece and we accepted happily. The idea was worth it. Sailing back downwind it took only two hours to get to Cruz Bay.

This was the first time we had been to this small capital of St. John, which had a few low red-corrugated-iron-roofed buildings tucked between the palms in a lush cove with a boatyard and a ferry dock beside a white beach. We anchored and rowed our charter party ashore. Bands were playing, stalls were selling food and native knickknacks, and I bought J. small black coral earrings with our charter fee. That night we lounged in our cockpit and watched the fireworks exploding over the harbor, and we wouldn't have felt more privileged if we had been aboard the Royal Yacht *Britannia*.

We liked St. John. It was small and unspoiled, entirely without the commercial buzz of St. Thomas, and being U.S. territory, we could work there. We needed to stay put for a while; there was much to be done on the new boat before we cruised it any distance, and we had to make some money.

I got a job at Caneel Bay, the dull and snooty Rockefeller-owned resort on the west coast of St. John, around the corner from Cruz Bay. I worked as a laborer at Caneel's own small boatyard in Cruz Bay which serviced its ferries that brought guests over from St. Thomas. We anchored only a few hundred yards off the boatyard, and J. rowed me ashore every morning. She spent her days working on *Magdalena*, painting and varnishing. She talked about looking for a job too, but while I was earning there was no urgent need. Most of what I made went to paint and varnish, thinner and glue, and each week we stuck a few more dollars in an envelope we kept stashed inside the saloon's little solid-fuel stove.

On weekends we sailed out of Cruz Bay and tacked to windward along St. John's north shore, learning more each time about our boat and how to sail it. We anchored in Maho Bay, a tiny palm-fringed beach that we usually had all to ourselves because the sailing guidebooks told cruisers to go to Francis Bay farther to the north, and obediently they did. We swam and hiked up through the rough bush in the hills to where we could see *Magdaleña* far below, and Tortola across Drake's Channel, and in the distance Jost Van Dyke and the Atlantic Ocean. We speared fish and ate dinner in the cockpit, admired our boat and talked of where we would go in it someday, and we watched the sun go down over St. Thomas— which looked pretty at a distance.

We got a little tabby kitty we named Minou from the Humane Society on St. Thomas, who tried immediately to escape and leaped overboard for the first and last time.

Anchored in Cruz Bay, among the native fishing boats and a few plastic daysailers, were four other small wooden boats with full-time live-aboards, all Americans in their late twenties, our age. We saw these people every day, rowing past one another's boats to and from shore; we drank beer and wine on one boat or other, and talked about boats and sailing. Tom Averna, from Massachusetts, who had a dense black beard and looked like a Greek in an ancient mural, had the prettiest boat, *Silver Seal*, a twenty-four-foot English gaff cutter. Alan Johnson's *Driftwood* was the roughest, a native craft he'd fixed up and painted fire-engine red; he was the best sailor among us and I got a few pointers from him. Stu, living aboard a homemade plywood boat, was a little older; he'd done time for some paper crime and was now on parole. Ed and Sue lived on a tiny wooden Folkboat, twenty-five feet long, and were unhappy. Ed was fat and sullen and treated pretty dark-haired Sue like a maid.

We weren't best friends, but we were all living the same life and shared the same dream—to take off, whether it was down-island or around the world—and we watched one another with interest to see how the other was going about it. We were poor, living hand-to-mouth, fixing up our boats, the two married couples trying to stay together, the two single guys trying to get laid. We were all, more or less, in the same boat.

In midsummer, Alan, who also worked in the Caneel boatyard

with me, heard of a course being given in Red Hook to study and take the exam for U.S. Coast Guard licenses. He and Tom and I signed up, and then J., not wanting to be left out and forever, it seemed, competing with me, signed up too. For the next week, after work, the four of us jumped into Alan's whaler and powered across lumpy Pillsbury Sound, past the rooted *Xanadu*, into Red Hook. We bought smoked marlin for our suppers at Johnny Harms's sportfishing marina and chewed it through our classes, and powered back to St. John in the dark, when fish would leap out of the water beside us. It was a cram course in the Coast Guard syllabus; we learned basic rules of the road, lights, signaling, elementary navigation, some stuff we knew, some we didn't. We all passed, and J. and I both scored 100.

Because of the time we claimed, backed up with some written testimonials, of work aboard several large yachts in the Mediterranean (J. had worked on a ferry in Mallorca), and our time on *Viva*, we were given U.S.C.G. hundred-ton Ocean Operator's licenses. At the Caneel boatyard there was resentment among some of the older ferry captains that we had come by our licenses with such apparent ease. I didn't care. It meant that I could drive the Caneel ferries—or any other boat as a professional—when a position opened up. I would get better money. And I would be a captain, no little thing in a boat-oriented world.

The turnover in boat-related jobs, filled as they usually are by boaters—a wandering breed—is high, and within a few weeks I was driving the ferries and enjoying, for a while, my exalted new status and paycheck. It was a dull job, like driving a bus, and I had little contact with my passengers. But the twenty-minute trip across Pillsbury Sound was always beautiful, and it kept me on the water, where I wanted to be. From the wheelhouse I used to see small white butterflies flying precariously from one island to the other, and I tried to avoid smashing into them. I would swerve the sixty-ton ferry when I could make them out ahead, and this eventually brought complaints from unseated passengers. I learned to gentle my swerves.

Caneel Bay was good to us. I was able to buy screws and nuts and bolts at cost from the boatyard, and to use the facilities there after hours or on weekends. I made a magazine rack for *Magdalena*'s saloon, a cutlery box for the galley, and a teak box for binoculars that I screwed to the bulkhead inside the companionway. When I became a captain and drove the ferries, I found myself elevated in the Caneel staff hierarchy and J. and I could now take tea with the guests and eat meals on the dining patio for cost, the most splendid of which was the twenty-five-foot-long Sunday buffet, which looked like the feast the Tahitians laid on for the *Bounty*'s crew, with the addition of baroque ice sculptures.

This should have been a good time for us, but instead J. and I seemed to start spiraling down toward a crash. After the first thrilling rush of independence we felt living aboard our boat, we grew steadily unhappier. We felt trapped, immobilized by a listless ennui, the lack of a plan, a want of discipline. We were lulled by our easy lifestyle, its absence of demands. We felt worthless because we were doing nothing and going nowhere. It is the common trap of the indolent tropics.

After a few months at Caneel Bay, I grew anxious coming home each day after work. J. had not found a job ashore. I was rowing myself in and out because she had no wish to leave the boat without me. Alone in the boat all day, anchored offshore, she was becoming severely isolated. She seldom felt like mixing with anyone else and didn't want me to go anywhere without her. She was plunging into depression and I was of little help to her. I wanted us to sail around the world, I lived and breathed the idea, read all the books I could find on the subject; but I also ranted about what a pokey wreck our boat was and talked about selling it and buying a cottage and growing organic vegetables. Or returning to London and getting back into advertising, making commercials, as Martin and my brother David were then doing. They were both living in London, seeing each other regularly, and I missed them. I felt left out and left behind. I lay around the boat thinking about life elsewhere. I felt trapped in J.'s narrowing cocoon and I wanted to get out.

Her diary toward the end of this second year of our marriage thins to cryptic, depressed remarks on odd days and is blank altogether for its last three months.

In the fall, at the humid, active end of the hurricane season, heavy rains flooded the islands with steaming mud, and the pellucid blue water in Pillsbury Sound turned to a thick brown equatorial soup filled with trash and flotsam. Instead of dodging butterflies, I had to steer the ferry around the bloated carcasses of goats that had washed out to sea. I grew tired of Caneel and my job, and our life in St. John had become isolated and claustrophobic for both of us. I wanted to try using my new license in the sailboat charter game, so we sailed back to St. Thomas and I began making the rounds of the bareboat charter companies.

A "bareboat" charter captain is an oxymoronic position, since a bareboat is one that charterers rent without a captain or crew; but often, if the charterers are inexperienced, the charter company requires that they take a captain along. Living on my own sailboat, with a big license, I appeared to qualify and I was soon sailing professionally, a week at a time, once every two or three weeks.

It was hardly work. The charterers wanted to do most of the sail-handling and steering. They would typically be a family, full of inside humor and friction, or two couples, or occasionally a mix of singles—stressed, anxious people, larval-white and slathered with sunblock. I'd take them from St. Thomas to Virgin Gorda and deliver them back a week later brown, relaxed, and usually much happier. I found, almost to my surprise, that it was rewarding work.

It also gave J. and me week-long breaks from each other, and the opportunity to miss and appreciate and look forward to seeing each other.

On my very first trip, I had never been beyond Tortola and disappeared frequently below to bone up on the next stretch or anchorage in *The Yachtsman's Guide to the Virgin Islands*. In time, I discovered which islands, anchorages, shoreside restaurants, and routes between them worked best and made for the happiest crew, and the forty-odd-mile trip up to Virgin Gorda and back became somewhat unvarying.

I soon got to know others going the same way, other bareboat skippers, and couples running their own private charter yachts, like Bruce and Sarah Comstock, former computer programmers from Boston who owned and lived aboard and chartered a fifty-foot fiberglass ketch, *Arawak*. I might introduce my charterers to theirs, or we might all find ourselves eating together at Stanley's in Canegarden Bay or the Virgin Gorda Yacht Club. They told me about the Tuesday night barbecue on the beach at Peter Island, put on by the yacht club there. This was the closest thing you'd find in the Virgin Islands to a luau, and Bruce and Sarah told me they always took their charterers there. I started fetching up at Peter Island on Tuesdays too.

Bruce was short, barrel-chested, bearded, bald, and always wore a hat. He was an unrelenting curmudgeon, scathing of his charterers and everybody else in the world out of earshot. He would tell long anecdotes illustrating the uselessness, the ineptitude, the low qualities of anybody you might mention. Sarah, on the other hand, was a peach. She was warm, compassionate, funny, very bright, and more than made up for Bruce. She was peach-colored too: dark blond hair, honey-and-peach skin, and I thought she was altogether beautiful. I rarely saw her and Bruce exchange a word. I never saw them touch each other.

It seemed to me that I often found a seat next to Sarah at the Peter Island barbecue, or that she was ready to swim ashore with me if I paddled past *Arawak*. She was intuitive, and probably knew I had trouble at home, and I saw the same was true with her. Soon, without saying much, we had gone a long way together on a few swims and meals ashore, all the while surrounded by Bruce and our happy charterers.

Our boat—for a few months at this time called *Coquelicot* in J.'s diary—was now anchored off the Sheraton Hotel and Marina at the edge of Charlotte Amalie. It was convenient to the charter companies I worked for, and J. had finally found work helping run the shoreside operation of one of these companies, which had its office right in the marina.

One night we were ashore in the marina bar when another boater from the anchorage rowed in to tell us that our boat had been wrecked. We jumped into our dinghy and rowed out to find it afloat but mastless, or so it seemed in the dark. In fact, the mast was lying horizontally on top of the boat, folded straight back from its tabernacle hinge on the cabin roof, supported at the stern by the smashed framework of the homemade wind vane, and sticking out another fifteen feet beyond. In the dark and crowded anchorage, the skipper of a much larger boat, equipped with a powerful anchor windlass, had raised his anchor, snagging ours without realizing it, breaking it out from the muddy bottom, and steamed off through the anchorage towing our boat and startled cat Minou astern. *Coquelicot* had slewed sideways, the bowsprit colliding with another boat, and the fitting on the end of the sprit, to which the forestay was attached, had broken. That was all that was holding up the mast—a thick, solid Scottish fir tree—which then simply fell backward with the full force of its dead weight. We discovered Minou burrowed deep in our bunk below, puffed up into a round freaked-out ball. After fifteen minutes in J.'s lap he was purring, his fur almost flattened to normal. But our life—bumpy as it may have been—was derailed for six months.

The boat that had pulled ours on its brief sleigh ride was fortunately insured (we were not). A settlement was worked out, and Billy Walker came in his launch and towed *Coquelicot* around the south shore of St. Thomas, back through the labyrinthine channels of the Lagoon, back to the boatyard where we had first seen it.

In addition to the accident damage, the boat also had a slew of preexisting problems that we had put up with or consigned to the someday: the cracked frames—we still weren't sure how many—that Newt Farley had pointed out when he'd performed his abbreviated survey; rusty rigging; rotten cordage; a series of leaks all over the roof and the decks, which brought miserable drips in the almost daily tropical downpours. And a galley—a crappy makeshift with a rusty stove, a discolored plastic sink, a pump that didn't want to deliver water—that we both hated. All this had been tolerable while we were anchored in clear blue water and had a characterful, if run-down, sailboat that we could take sailing. Now we were towed back into the Lagoon, wrecked and squalid.

The dock where we tied up at Antilles Yacht Services was almost exclusively filled with other wooden boats in states of terminal renovation. Owned by young couples like ourselves who had bought them because they were run-down and cheap, these projects had become an all-consuming lifestyle. The typical boat had a cockpit filled with rusty tools, pots of paint, tubes of glue and caulking. The male owner, in cutoffs and a glue-caked T shirt, was seen, or heard, contorted inside some locker or the bilge, banging and grunting, or sitting at the grounded hulk of the Pinafore bar, which sat directly at the head of the dock, with a Heineken in his hand talking with another renovation dreamer about sailing down-island in just another few months. In the evenings, his mate would appear, wet-haired from the scummy boatyard shower, but pretty in a skirt and frilly island top, setting off for her job as a waitress. She supported the effort financially and applied the paint and varnish, while her husband/boyfriend/captain did the "skilled" work: the planking, the refastening, the mystical application of epoxy glue, gutting the entire interior and rebuilding the new and vastly improved arrangement, and knocking back greenies at the bar in the company of fellow experts.

We had seen these same boats and people here a year earlier when we had bought our boat and sailed away. Without exception, the projects all appeared to have regressed until they looked like the early stages of new construction using recycled materials. The story was always the same:

"Well, man, like, we figured if we were going to glass the cockpit we might as well do the decks at the same time, and, you know, the decks were shot anyway."

"Once we got the paint off we found some rot and we had to put in the new planking. But man, she'll be stronger than new."

"Well, you know, once we got this far we decided . . ."

These people had all run hard aground. They did not look up from their glue joints. They were embarked on curves of effort that bent farther from their dreamed-of ends the longer they worked. They became lost in the details, and the projects mired in cost and heartache. Couples split up, the first mate usually disappearing back to the States, the captain left with the rotting ship, and soon some sweet new mate would buy into the dream, or need a place to crash, and on it would go.

We looked around, we looked at our wrecked boat, we looked at ourselves, and we knew we were *that close* to the same scenario. With this specter before us, J. and I joined forces with unspoken, unswerving agreement and went to work. It was, for a while, the making of us.

We too decided that if we were stuck here for a time doing major work, we might as well do as much as possible at once. But we would not languish here. This was not our idea of Caribbean utopia. The Lagoon water was brown and murky, particularly around the community dock: the plumbing system aboard boats was either a marine loo that pumped its contents straight into the water next to your boat, or, for those renovating the head, a bucket. The mangrove swamps creating and encircling the Lagoon to seaward shut out the breeze, hindered the circulation and exchange of water, and bred billions of mosquitoes. Yet Antilles Yacht Services had the facilities we needed, and it had Billy Walker, a testy, harassed Englishman a little older than me, who would for some reason always stop his work to tell me or show me how to do something, and come aboard and see how I'd done it and shake his head in grim, pitying encouragement. Billy was worth the price of admission.

I still went off chartering. J. quit the charter office and began waitressing evenings in a nearby restaurant. We weren't making a lot of money, but it was all cash and the bulk of it, and all our time not spent working, went into the boat. Compared to the other boats at the dock, ours transformed like a flower growing in time-lapse photography.

This is what we did to our boat: We found seventy-five cracked oak frames between stem and stern, enough to indicate a rough grounding at some point in the past, and together a serious weakness. Billy Walker showed me how to laminate "sister" frames— thin, bendable strips of Douglas fir nailed and epoxy-glued one on top of the other—alongside the cracked ones, temporarily secured to the hull with little boatnails. When we later hauled the boat out of the water, each frame was fastened through the hull planking from the outside with twelve bronze screws—nine hundred altogether, screwed in with a hand brace in one weekend.

We tore the delaminating, leaking canvas off the entire decks and cabin top, sanded down the bare wood beneath, and replaced it with fiberglass and resin. Our deck leaks stopped absolutely, and we whooped and grinned at each other inside our boat when the next rains came.

We gutted the inside of the hull aft of the saloon and built in a new galley and chart table. We got a deal from a charter company on a three-burner gas stove, with grill and oven, which we gimballed so that it would remain flat when the boat heeled. We had no engine, so we built in a mass of stowage room aft and beneath the galley.

A beautiful old mahogany Chris Craft cabin cruiser lay rotting at the boatyard, its owner long gone with unpaid bills. The night before the yard bulldozed it into scrap wood, Norman, a renovation dreamer, and I crawled over it from end to end with screwdrivers and wrenches and came away with armfuls of bronze cleats, naval pipes, hasps, latches, and other arcane bits of bronze hardware too wonderful to leave behind.

We heard of a German blacksmith in Sub Base (site of the former U.S. Navy submarine base west of Charlotte Amalie) and went to see him about replacing the boat's old galvanized but now rusting bowsprit and bumkin cranse irons and chainplates. Dieter was a very small, slight man who dressed in pale pink or blue shorts and shirt that made him look like a schoolboy. He rode a bicycle everywhere. A sixty-five-foot-long aluminum yacht was nearing completion outside the front of his shop, built entirely by himself. I showed Dieter our old rusty bits and pieces and he knew immediately what he was dealing with. He said "*Ja, ja, ja,* von of zose boats," and he made new ones, on the spot, in stainless steel, and charged me only the stock weight of the metal. He left these fabrications rough and sharp and gave me a file, pushed me toward a vise, and checked on me as I smoothed the rough edges. Then he polished all this new hardware with a fine carbide grinder until it looked like silver sculpture. Finally, he took me aboard his own boat a-building. Along with everything else aboard, he proudly pointed out the artwork: a ghastly print of an old mariner in sou'wester smoking a pipe which he had bought at Woolworth's.

Billy Walker scooped the deep crack out of our mast and scarfed in a fir "dutchman." J. and I sanded down the mast and put ten coats of varnish on it.

We replaced all the old galvanized rigging with new stainless steel wire, tightened it up with new bronze turnbuckles ordered from England, and bolted Dieter's new chainplates to the hull. I rebuilt the wind vane. We bought fifty fathoms of new anchor chain. We bolted and bedded new mahogany toerails and rubrails the whole length of the boat at the joint of the hull and deck, and new teak trim pieces to the cabin roof, and varnished them all. We painted the whole boat again, inside and out.

"Wow, man," everybody on the dock said, in slightly hurt tones.

When we were nearly finished, the boat looked as we had long imagined it might. It still wasn't a sleek or classically pretty craft, yet it had a characterful, purposeful look that we both now liked. But enough with the pretty names, we decided. The strong, seaworthy-looking phoenix that rose from this rebuild was called, finally, *Toad*. J. painted this name on the stern—the first time we had done this—and after that it never occurred to us to change our minds again. People who had known the boat before and saw it now didn't recognize it and thought it was a new arrival in the islands. "Look at *Toad*," we heard people say, and it sounded right to us.

We were out of the Lagoon in six months. We sailed back to St. John, where we could dive overboard into clear water and where we had no fears of being Lagooned forever. Our boat looked, at last, to our eyes, beautiful. And we were looking much better to each other.

We started cruising in our born-again *Toad*. Seeing our "new" boat through the eyes of people close to us, and their appreciation of it, rekindled our desire to sail farther afield, and also gave us our happiest cruises in the Virgin Islands.

David flew out from England to see us, fresh from his first experience as a producer (of a Lipton tea commercial for Arab-speaking television networks in the Middle East: scenes of chic, blue-jeaned Arab youths who were hip and foresightful enough to carry a Lipton tea bag around in their back pockets). He spent three weeks with us, and we all agreed afterward it was the best vacation any of us ever had. We sailed *Toad* up the well-trod highway to Virgin Gorda, hitting all the piña colada joints I had taken charterers to on the way. We rented motorcycles on Tortola; we swam, snorkeled, and spearfished. We sailed through crowded anchorages and current-ripped cuts as if we knew exactly what we were doing. Then we sailed across the Anegada Passage—a small overnight voyage, a taste of wider seafaring—to the French island of St. Barts, where we stuffed ourselves with *patisseries, baguettes, pâté*. David fell in love with *Toad*, which now seemed an able, comfortable, trusty magic carpet. And J. and I now seemed able to sail it with skill, even some dash.

When he left, we found we'd spent all our money. I went back to work, and J. now began to make use of her license, skippering charter boats when large parties hired two or three boats at a time and we cruised in tandem up to Virgin Gorda and back. These skippering jobs were good for her self-confidence; she was happy, she looked beautiful, the charterers all thought she was incredible— and she was. I wondered at my luck in having such a woman, and grew full of hope again.

We met Thom and Beth Wilson when they anchored their small, well-prepared fiberglass thirty-footer next to us for several days in Cruz Bay. A lean couple our age, they were making a year-long circuit of the Caribbean from Florida and back. We quickly became friends and had a Thanksgiving feast together aboard *Toad*.

We spent two weeks sailing slowly up through the islands in company with them, eating supper together on one boat or another, spearfishing, and taking long walks. They were, at that moment in time, what we hoped we could become: a tight unit on a tight boat, outward bound. For all four of us, our minds and attitudes clicked powerfully together. J. and I climbed up to the top of Mosquito Island when they sailed onward to the south, and miserably watched them disappear beyond Virgin Gorda.

But Thom and Beth galvanized us. We were impressed by the planning and execution of their cruise, and by the performance of *Toad* alongside their boat—they beat us always in their modern design, but not badly; for all intents and purposes, we had kept up with them. We decided we would leave the Virgin Islands, where we had been for two and a half years, and sail away. *Toad* was ready. We were stale. It was time to go. We decided to sail as far as Florida. There we could work again, build up a good cruising kitty, and sail on, either east across the Atlantic or west, through Panama, to the Pacific.

We told our friends and made our preparations. On one of my last charters, Sarah Comstock and I were sitting next to each other at the barbecue on Peter Island one Tuesday night, when she said to me: "I want you to know that I care about you."

She said it in a firm, quiet way that made me think she might even care about me as much as I cared about her. "I care about you too," I said. I saw *Arawak* a few more times, but we never had a chance to say anything more to each other.

A few weeks later, J. and I sailed away for Florida.

July 21

We are becalmed. Then we ghost on zephyrs for a few hours until we lie rolling slightly and stopped again. I feel the mind-boggling enormity of the ocean as I crawl across it at often less than a walking pace. I can see it on my fifty-three-inch-wide chart of the North Atlantic on which my daily X's are half an inch apart. I feel smaller than a *Physalia*. As lonely as a satellite—an astronaut in outer space is in closer touch with the world than I am, with forty people in Houston monitoring every burp.

The greatest reward of sailing alone (that I have discovered so far) is that no one comes between you and the indescribably beautiful world around you. You experience it directly without the muddying filter of someone else's impression. At moments, standing on deck looking at the lonely sea and the sky, you find yourself moved to a mix of joy and sadness that breaks your heart. But it's at just these moments that you also find yourself wanting to share it all with someone you love.

1830: I feel very far away from everything and everyone I love today.

I wake in the middle of the night and it is as if the wind has been waiting for me to appear, groggy in the hatchway. We are still becalmed, but within seconds I feel it on my cheek, a breath from the south. By starlight I see it coming across the water on my left like the shadow of a cloud moving across a field, mottling the flat calm mirror on which we have been sitting, turning the surface dark and opaque.

The breeze builds, then steadies into a light wind that I somehow believe in. This is the leading edge of something extending across a broad reach of ocean, I feel, with all the intuition I've acquired in place of a weatherfax machine. I believe—I fervently hope with the excitement of a pioneer in a prairie schooner passing over the continental divide and seeing the downslope—that we have at this instant sailed out of the windless mid-ocean high into the prevailing pattern of southwesterlies blowing alongside the American continent. This is our wind that will take us to the shore. It fills the main and genoa, which have been loose and flapping for days, weeks it seems. Now they are quiet, filled with wind like kites, pulling *Toad* through the air. After almost three weeks at sea, lurching, rolling, and pitching, I feel no movement at all now—save for a slight, delicious acceleration—as the boat stiffens and we glide across the flat ocean surface. It is so thrilling I can't go right back to sleep. I stay up for the ride.

Within an hour it is blowing twelve knots, a real breeze. The crests of waves are breaking into small phosphorescent whitecaps. This is perfect sailing. I've seen nothing like this since before the Azores. We are bombing along at five knots, pointing at Cape Cod, 1,300 miles away.

Anxiety drains out me. We're on our way at last. I go below to sleep.

July 22

At 0500, just before dawn, the alarm wakes me. Swinging my feet off the bunk, I touch water before floor.

Real panic. Before I know it I'm up in the cockpit pumping for all I'm worth—so frenziedly that part of my mind is wondering about the age and strength left in the sun-faded rubber diaphragm C-clamped on the pump's exterior. I have a spare, but it would rattle me further if this broke and I had to repair it right now. Pump-pump-pump-pump-pump-pump. After a while—I've forgotten to count or look at my watch—I look down the companionway: water's no longer visible over the wet floorboards. I slow down a bit, catch my breath. Several deep breaths. What a way to wake up!

I start thinking: I was in the lee bunk—the lower side of the boat now that it's well heeled with wind in the sails for the first time in weeks. Water just under the floor when the boat is becalmed and upright would overflow on the lee side when moving and heeled. No need for panic. But water over the floorboards is above the threshold of my peace of mind.

Five minutes later I know with certainty there's a shitload more water coming in now. Still no suck from the bilge and I've been at it for ten minutes at least. I stop and go below and pull up a floorboard. The bilge appears half full. Je-sus *Christ*.

Up in the cockpit I pump like a mad metronome. Of course, I think, the bilge is V-shaped so what looks half full is really probably only a quarter full. I normally see half a glass of water as half full, but I have just become a fervent half-empty man.

Another five minutes until I hear the sucking of air from bilge. I go below, up into the bow, and what I see is a waking nightmare that makes my gut feel suddenly full of ice: water is welling in, steadily, along half the seams in the hull below the waterline, on both sides. The inside of the planking up here looks as if a hose is being played across it. I pull sails, duffel bags, coils of rope wildly away from the hull to see how far aft this continues. Not far, thank God, not too far: it stops about six feet or so back from the stem. The planking is dry aft of this. The water's getting under the sheathing, of course, and coming in through the seams, which haven't been caulked for a decade at least. You can't caulk them if you can't get at them, but the water sure can. I stare for a few minutes, trying to think—of what, I don't know. Through the hatch light overhead I can see that it's dawn.

I go aft and start making coffee.

Okay. I can still pump it out, I can keep it below the floor-boards. But no question about it now: the faster I sail, the more water comes in. However, we're doing about five knots now, we won't go much faster than this, so maybe it'll stabilize at this rate.

Not a hope. The leak got progressively worse over the last two weeks while we were practically sitting still. It will get worse and worse, faster and faster, and I know why now: the water will work away at the old caulking and force its way aft. It's a race against time.

But aren't we moving well!

I think of the Alitalia joke a Pan Am flight attendent once told me: An announcement from the cockpit: "We gotta good news, anda bad news. The bad news is we're lost. The good news is, we're makinga great time."

Later in the morning, the liquid crystal digital display on my short-wave radio starts fragmenting: batteries are low. I change them, but when I turn the radio back on it is silent. A second moment of raw panic this morning. Absurdly, this seems far worse than the leak. The prospect of life without my radio makes me feel lonelier than Robinson Crusoe. The radio is my man Friday, my contact with the rest of the species. Auntie BBC, jazz from the VOA in the evenings, this is the company that has kept me from feeling utterly alone.

I pull the batteries, brand-new Duracells, out of the radio and look at the contact points inside the battery compartment. Nice and shiny, no sign of corrosion. The batteries, fresh from their plastic packaging, look good too. I put them back, slowly, firmly, with the intense telepathic message: *You will work now.* I put the lid back on. Turn the radio on—

Nothing.

I unscrew the back of the radio and pull it off, revealing the inscrutable Japanese interior. I might as well be looking at an atomic bomb. I see no sign of corrosion, which I could expect after years on board. I pick the radio up and turn it upside down: nothing falls out, which is good, but then I realize that if it had I wouldn't know where it came from to put it back. Miserably, I screw the back on.

I feel a terrible cascading fear. I'm undermined, no doubt, by the other, realistically greater problem, but I am undone by the silence from my radio. I feel myself reverting to the baby state I escaped into on the dope boat: I want to blubber and appeal to someone, *"Pleeeeaaase!"* More than a thousand miles to go, ten to fifteen days. Cut off from the world. Absolutely, completely, out-of-touch alone.

Almost whimpering, I climb into the cockpit and start pumping. Pump-pump-pump. The voyage seems too grim now. Suddenly it's no longer fun. I look around at the empty ocean and realize, with a sharpness I've never felt before, how alone I am. Just myself and a leaky boat in the middle of the ocean. Alone, alone, all, all alone.

But isn't this really what you've wanted all along? A real test? To see if you can take it? This is now, at last, a survival situation, mentally and physically. It's perfect. It's going to take everything you've got. Are you going to cave in now, as you did once before, on the *Mary Nell*, when someone else was looking after you, or are you going to rise to this? If you set out across an ocean in a boat like *Toad*, eager for a whiff of danger and sensation but unprepared to face just such a scenario, you're just a fucking dilettante. This is real. Life or death. Are you up to it, or not?

Why are you here?

In 1966–7, sixty-five-year-old Englishman Francis Chichester sailed alone around the world. He stopped only once, in Australia, for seven weeks, to rest up for the long second leg by way of Cape Horn, and to give interviews, building public interest in his voyage, for he was a canny publicist. He was a tall, thin, geeky-looking old bloke, with Coke-bottle glasses, and a cap bearing the Pure Wool trademark, the logo of his British Wool sponsors. The reason Chichester gave for making the voyage was to see if a modern yacht could beat the round-the-world sailing times of the old clipper ships plying between England and Australia along their now obsolete route. This route was south from England, down the Atlantic, then east through an ocean not found on any map but known to sailors as the Southern Ocean: the empty windswept stretches of the Atlantic, Pacific, and Indian Oceans at the bottom of the world, between latitudes 40 and 50 degrees south. A place also known as the "Roaring Forties" and the "Furious Fifties," where storm-force westerly winds drove great ships at their maximum speed. These winds develop huge seas that roll around the globe like an unceasing formation of tsunamis, unimpeded by land except in one place, Cape Horn, the southernmost rock of the Andes, the scorpion tail tip of South America. Once around the Horn—if they made it around—ships would turn north and head back up the Atlantic, to England.

A small modern yacht against great old ships. An essentially pointless accomplishment (and, in fact, Chichester failed to smash any old clipper ship records), but it carried the specious ring of a worthy endeavor. The real reason Chichester went was that he was an adventurer: as a young man he had made a pioneering flight in a small aircraft from England to Australia; he had raced other single-handed sailors across the Atlantic; and now, in his sixties, he was still unable to sit at home and be done with adventuring. As to where he went, his route, there was a much more compelling reason than beating clipper ship times (although this provided an interesting measure of his time): this east-about route around the world, by way of the Forties and the Horn, is the fastest, the most fearful, the most dangerous way to sail around the world. It is Everest for sailors. Chichester went that way because it was there.

For England, sadly reduced in world stature since World War II, with no plucky British astronauts, a "brain drain" of its premier scientists and thinkers decamping to America for more money, its only great twentieth century heroes being Hillary (a New Zealander) of Everest, and Scott, the epic Antarctic bungler whose heroic posturing and ineptitude killed himself and his party, Chichester filled a famished void. No one had done what he had done. A quarter of a million people lined Plymouth Harbor the evening in May 1967 when he sailed home. Later he sailed on to Greenwich, in London, stepped ashore, and knelt before Queen Elizabeth, who dubbed his shoulders with a sword and knighted him on the spot. Both events were nationally televised. I remember sitting in front of the telly in London, watching, sixteen years old and not quite sure what he'd done or what all the fuss was about.

Among others watching was, no doubt, Robin Knox-Johnston, sixteen miles from where I was watching in London, if he was at his parents' home in Downe, Kent, where he was living at the time:

"I see that Tabarly is building a trimaran," my father said one morning. "Would that be suitable for the Transatlantic race?" . . .

"I wouldn't have thought so," I said. "Are there any other details?"

"No, but I wonder if he is going to try and beat Chichester's time, or perhaps even go round non-stop. That's about all there's left to do now, isn't it?"

He got up and left for the office, leaving me stirring a cup of coffee and thinking. "That's about all there's left to do now" kept turning in my mind. Going non-stop around the world *was* all that was left to be done in the sailing marathons. Chichester had stopped in Australia. . . . Who would try going round non-stop singlehanded? It would only be a matter of time. . . .

So begins Knox-Johnston's book. This conversation took place in March 1967, two months before Chichester returned. Within a month, Knox-Johnston was talking with a yacht designer about having a boat designed specifically for a nonstop circumnavigation—a boat which ultimately he couldn't afford, leaving *Suhaili*, which he already owned, as his only option.

Chichester's voyage provoked the same thought in others. By the end of 1967, at least six men were making plans for nonstop circumnavigations. The London *Sunday Times*, which had partially sponsored Chichester and covered his story—hesitantly at first, then enthusiastically as Chichestermania rose to a frenzy—got wind of the nonstop gang, all of whom were contacting newspapers seeking sponsorship. The *Sunday Times* grabbed the initiative away from its Fleet Street competitors by formalizing these efforts with the announcement, in March 1968, of its Golden Globe Race. It would award a prize of a trophy, a "golden globe," to the first single-handed sailor to circumnavigate nonstop—from England, to England. For the sailor making the fastest voyage there would be a cash prize of £5,000. For these sailors, the sole purpose in going was to be first; the cash prize, unless the first man was also the fastest, would be a bitter consolation. What these sailors wanted most in all the world was that kitschy golden globe.

The first to sail, on June 1, 1968, was John Ridgway, a twenty-nine-year-old captain in the Special Air Service (England's premier

SWAT commando group: the chaps in black they call in to rappel down a rope from the roof of a terrorist-occupied embassy, smash in through the windows, and save the hostage secretaries). Ridgway had already been to sea: in 1966 he had rowed across the Atlantic from Cape Cod to Ireland with a Scottish paratrooper, Chay Blyth. Two unquestionably tough men. Not to be left behind, Blyth set out after him on June 8. Both men were sailing stock thirty-foot-long fiberglass cruising boats, the sort in which a young family might poke about the Isle of Wight for the weekend, totally unsuitable for the Southern Ocean. As Ridgway left port, a twenty-five-ton vessel loaded with TV cameras collided with his little boat, smashing some woodwork, but he sailed on.

Ridgway knew how to sail; Chay Blyth did not. He took some lessons before leaving, but required help raising and setting his sails on the day of departure, and followed friends on another boat out of port, copying their maneuvers. Three weeks later, in a gale that was only a hint of what he would face in the Southern Ocean, he found his shallow-drafted boat unmanageable. He lowered the sails and went below, where he prayed and read sailing manuals, feeling, he later wrote, as if he was in hell with instructions.

Knox-Johnston left next, on June 14, from Falmouth. He was followed, on August 22, by two Frenchmen (who first had to sail north to England, to leave from a British port, to be eligible for the *Sunday Times* prizes): Loïck Fougeron, in a thirty-foot steel cutter, and Bernard Moitessier, in his forty-foot-long steel ketch, *Joshua*. Moitessier, forty-three years old, was by far the most formidable competitor, already legendary in small-boat voyaging circles. Born in Vietnam, he had grown up sailing junk-rigged sampans. In 1965–6 he had sailed *Joshua* 14,216 miles nonstop, with his wife, from Tahiti to Spain via Cape Horn, at that time the longest nonstop voyage in a small sailboat. He had been there, he had done it. *Joshua* had been built with immense strength by a builder of commercial steel vessels, it was thoroughly tested, and Moitessier knew his boat intimately.

Moitessier had written two literate, rather mystical books about his already long life at sea, *Un Vagabond des Mers du Sud*, and *Cap Horn à la Voile*. The last covered his Tahiti–Cape Horn–Spain voyage, and in it he described a controversial technique he had discovered for surviving the monster storm seas in the Southern Ocean. As Hiscock writes in *Voyaging Under Sail*: "In 1966 something happened to shake the long-accepted theory of small craft management in heavy weather." This theory was essentially to reduce sail and heave-to—stopping, in effect—or to slow the yacht down by dragging a sea anchor (a submersible conical device) or long ropes weighted down with anchors or even tires. Moitessier's radical tactic was to run before the storm at full speed and surf down the face of giant overtaking waves at a slight angle. He claimed that surfing at angles of between 15 and 20 degrees prevented the boat from either rolling over sideways or somersaulting bow-over-stern.

Hiscock goes on:

A year after this event I took part in a *Yachting World* forum, in which four of us, including my old friend Adlard Coles—perhaps the most widely experienced British ocean-racing man of the day, and whose latest book, *Heavy Weather Sailing*, had recently been published—discussed yacht management in heavy weather. Naturally the Moitessier method cropped up, and we all found it rather startling. Coles said he had never dared try it.

Although Moitessier left England almost three months after Robin Knox-Johnston, *Joshua*'s greater length and speed, and Moitessier's reputation as a seaman, gave him every possibility, even probability, of catching up, overtaking, and winning.

On August 24, the oldest man in the race, fifty-eight-year-old Royal Navy Commander Bill King, set sail on what was supposed to be the ideal boat, one built specially for this race. Another Royal

Navy Commander, Nigel Tetley, sailed on September 16, in a forty-foot trimaran, a multihull design capable of greater speeds than any of the other boats, all monohulls, and theoretically, capable of over-taking them all and winning.

The eighth competitor was Donald Crowhurst. An ambitious electrical engineer, inventor, and weekend sailor, he had become convinced he could equip a trimaran with his own electronic inventions and beat everybody in the race. A charismatic, persuasive man, he found backers, although late in the day, to fund him and have a boat built for the race. But he got away very late, on the thirty-first of October, and only then because he was under the gun of a *Sunday Times* deadline. His boat was unfinished, untested, most of his inventions and ideas unimplemented. Crowhurst's charm, imagination, and ambition, fueled by an angry sense of thwarted superiority, got him to the starting gate, but he should not have gone. And in the end, the night before he left, he surely knew it:

> Donald and Clare [his wife] rowed out to the boat for a final inspection. It was still smothered with piled-up equipment. They sorted out as much as they could and then, at two in the morning, went back to the hotel. Once in bed, Donald lay silent beside Clare. After struggling for the right words, he finally said, in a very quiet voice: "Darling, I'm very disappointed in the boat. She's not right. I'm not prepared. If I leave with things in this hopeless state will you go out of your mind with worry?" Clare, in her turn, could only reply with another question. "If you give up now," she said, "will you be unhappy for the rest of your life?"
>
> Donald did not answer, but started to cry. He wept until morning. During that last night he had less than five minutes' sleep. "I was such a fool!" says Clare Crowhurst now. "Such a stupid fool! With all the evidence in front of me, I still didn't realize Don was telling me he'd failed, and wanted me to stop him."

This quote is from my British Penguin edition of *The Strange Voyage of Donald Crowhurst*, by Nicholas Tomalin and Ron Hall (who, at the time of the race, was the assistant editor of the *Sunday Times*). On the back it says: "The twisted epic of a man who sailed single-handed over the horizon of sanity."

The last competitor, Italian Alex Carozzo, also sailed on the October 31 deadline, in a brand-new, purpose-built sixty-six-footer, which, like Crowhurst's boat, was unfinished.

Ridgway and Blyth, lonely and demoralized when their weekend sailboats began to show the stress of ocean sailing, dropped out early on. Loïck Fougeron and Bill King were 380 miles apart in the South Atlantic when both had their yachts rolled over by the same storm. The masts were snapped off King's boat; Fougeron suffered no severe damage, but was frightened and knew then he didn't want to face what awaited him in the Southern Ocean. Both withdrew from the race. Soon after his late start, Alex Carozzo began vomiting blood from what appeared to be a hemor-rhaging ulcer and sailed no farther than Oporto, Portugal.

By December 1968, six months after setting out, Knox-Johnston was already past New Zealand, heading for Cape Horn, with Moitessier somewhere behind him—not far enough, he was sure. He had continued through an unending series of setbacks, which included the smashing of his self-steering wind vane (a homemade affair very similar to mine on *Toad*), a wave knocking *Suhaili*'s cabin roof askew, and sewing his mustache to a sail. He had considered giving up several times but had continued as long as he could find a way to do so.

Far behind—about 12,000 miles behind, and still in the Atlantic—the two trimarans followed. Nigel Tetley was doing poorly, averaging only 68 miles a day. But Donald Crowhurst, in the same sort of boat, appeared to be doing far better. On December 10 he radio-cabled his press agent in England that he had just sailed 243 miles in a single twenty-four-hour period. This appeared to be a record. Crowhurst was suddenly the lead in the *Sunday Times*'s next installment on the race:

CROWHURST SPEED WORLD RECORD?

Donald Crowhurst, last man out in the *Sunday Times* round-the-world lone-man yacht race, covered a breathtaking and possibly record-breaking 243 miles in his 41 foot trimaran Teignmouth Electron last Sunday. The achievement is even more remarkable in the light of the very poor speeds in the first three weeks of his voyage; he took longer to reach the Cape Verdes than any other competitor.

What Crowhurst had done to boost his poor performance, and put himself in the spotlight, was to begin to lie. From this point on, he radioed back to England increasingly exaggerated positions. In the newspaper maps, and in the minds of most people following the story, he now leaped ahead in a series of dazzling runs. He shot far past his real position, and in order to make this at all credible, he was forced to make up and maintain a fraudulent navigational record, a second set of books. As Hall and Tomalin note in *The Strange Voyage of Donald Crowhurst*: "His forgery is, in many ways, the most impressive bit of technical expertise of the entire voyage. To calculate backwards from an imagined distance to a series of daily positions, and from them via declination and other tables to the correct sun-sightings is a formidable and unfamiliar job, far harder than honest navigation."

Most people accepted Crowhurst's claims. But Sir Francis Chichester phoned the *Sunday Times* to say that Crowhurst had to be "a bit of a joker," and the *Times*'s navigational consultant for the race, Captain Craig Rich, of the London School of Navigation, expressed "considerable surprise."

Crowhurst had gambled everything on this voyage. Financially, he faced ruin if he did not at least win the £5,000 cash prize for the fastest voyage, and do well enough to generate a lot more than that in book sales and endorsements. He had also nailed his personality to this cross. He had postured to everyone, but most of all to himself, as the sort of bluff, patriotic, English adventurer who could pull off this epic caper. He wasn't.

But there is no doubt that this is exactly what Robin Knox Johnston is. No demonic neuroses for him. His heroes, often invoked in his book, are Elizabethan England's seadog adventurers, Drake and Frobisher, who sailed for gold and the glory of their queen—at least that's what English schoolboys are told. Here is his account of his Christmas aboard *Suhaili* in the Southern Ocean:

> Two glasses later I clambered out on deck and perched myself on the cabin top to hold a Carol Service. I sang happily away for over an hour, roaring out all my favorite carols. . . . At 3pm my time I drank a Loyal Toast, wishing that I had been up early enough to hear the Queen's speech at 6am my time. Somehow, gathering to listen to this speech adds to the charm of Christmas.

That evening on the radio he heard about Apollo 8 going around the moon and thought about the differences between their voyage and his own:

> I was doing absolutely nothing to advance scientific knowledge; I would not know how to. . . . True, once Chichester . . . had shown that this trip was possible, I could not accept that anyone but a Briton should be the first to do it, and I wanted to be that Briton. But nevertheless to my mind there was still an element of selfishness in it. My mother, when asked for her opinion of the voyage before I sailed, had replied that she considered it "totally irresponsible" and on this Christmas Day I began to think she was right. I was sailing round the world simply

because I bloody well wanted to—and, I realized, I was thoroughly enjoying myself.

A psychiatrist who saw him before and after the voyage, described him as "distressingly normal." I'm not sure normal is the word, considering the strength of his extraordinary resolve. He might worry about his boat, he might modestly belittle his voyage, but he had not a shred of self-doubt.

Crowhurst was a different sort altogether, made of frailer, darker stuff. As he sailed south down the Atlantic, his fake positions grew farther and farther away, in seas he was never to sail to: the Indian, the Pacific Ocean. He sailed toward Cape Horn, as if to turn around there and head for home—not at the head of the pack, for even with his false positions he was too far behind Knox-Johnston, but he could give everyone a run for their money making the fastest voyage and pick up the cash.

On January 17, 1969, Robin Knox-Johnston rounded Cape Horn.

> My first impulse . . . was to keep on going east. The feeling of having got past the worst was terrific and I suppose this impulse was a way of cocking a snook at the Southern Ocean itself, almost as if to say, "I've beaten you and now I'll go round again to prove it." Fortunately this phase passed very quickly. . . . I thought of hot baths, pints of beer, the other sex and steaks and turned up into the Atlantic for home.

At this point, Bernard Moitessier, sailing 20 percent faster, was only nineteen days behind him. It seemed possible that the two men could race up the Atlantic and reach England, after 30,000 miles and ten and a half months, in a photo finish.

The Frenchman was as unlike the Englishman as two men can be. It would appear, from his book about the race, *The Long Way*, that Moitessier spent at least half the voyage standing on deck, spiritually and sensually intoxicated, absorbing the elements around him by means of a mystical osmosis. So deep is his communion with the ocean and its creatures, that a pack of porpoises comes to warn him as *Joshua* bears down on New Zealand and takes a wrong turn:

> A tight line of 25 porpoises swimming abreast goes from stern to stem on the starboard side, in three breaths, then the whole group veers right and rushes off at right angles, all the fins cutting the water together and in the same breath taken on the fly. . . . I watch, wonderstruck. . . . Something pulls me, something pushes me. I look at the compass. *Joshua* [steered by wind vane] is running downwind at 7 knots straight for Stewart Island, hidden in the stratus. The steady west wind had shifted around to the south without my realizing it.

Moitessier then alters course, back onto a safe heading.

> And then something wonderful happens: a big black and white porpoise jumps ten or twelve feet in the air in a fantastic somersault, with two complete rolls. . . . Three times he does his double roll, bursting with a tremendous joy, as if he were shouting to me and all the other porpoises: "The man understood that we were trying to tell him to sail to the right . . . you understood . . . you understood . . . keep on like that, it's all clear ahead!"

You might pooh-pooh such a thing, if you didn't know about Pelorus Jack. Pelorus, the Latin name of the pilot of Hannibal's ship, is the name given to a nautical device for taking bearings. Pelorus Jack was a porpoise that swam about off French Pass, New Zealand, in the nineteenth century. He met all ships approaching the pass and piloted them through its maze of rocks. One day, a passenger aboard a ship pulled out a pistol and shot Pelorus Jack, for sport. The porpoise was wounded but recovered. He continued to meet ships off French Pass, with the sole exception of the ship that carried the passenger who shot him.

After rounding the Horn, Moitessier too felt an impulse to keep going east—and he did. He never turned left.

He carried no radio. His method of communicating his position to the *Sunday Times*, and his thoughts to the outside world, was to lob by slingshot small plastic containers with notes inside them onto the decks of passing ships. The first news of his decision came from Cape Town, where he lobbed a note to the *Sunday Times* onto the bridge of a tanker anchored in Table Bay as he sailed past. "The Horn was rounded February 5, and today is March 18. I am continuing non-stop towards the Pacific Islands because I am happy at sea, and perhaps also to save my soul."

He had decided that he had little interest in continuing back to Europe to win a race. "Leaving from Plymouth and returning to Plymouth now seems like leaving from nowhere to go nowhere," he writes in his book.

He was happy aboard *Joshua*, and felt he could go on forever. The privations of a long voyage didn't trouble him. It had been six months since he had bathed, back in the doldrums of the Atlantic. His hair had turned into dreadlocks: "My hair has grown so long it tangles on top of my head; the comb has not been able to run through it for several weeks. I thought I had got tar on my hair."

When the news reached England that Moitessier had kept on going, it was widely assumed he had gone barmy. Whatever his state of mind, it worked for him. He sailed on to Tahiti, arriving there on June 21, 1969, ten months after leaving Plymouth. He wrote *The Long Way*, which became a best-seller in France, remarried, and started a new family.

It would have been a close race indeed if he had continued on to England. Knox-Johnston calculated that theoretically he would still have won:

Moitessier would have been slowed in the Variables and the Doldrums just as I was, but even if one ignores this and allows him his full average speed of 117 miles a day all the way home . . . he would in theory still have had fifty miles to go to Plymouth on the day that I arrived in Falmouth.

Fifty miles is just ten hours' sailing.

Moitessier is far better remembered for going on than he ever would have been for coming in second.

Knox-Johnston sailed into Falmouth, amid a flotilla of welcoming boats, on April 22, after 313 days at sea.

There remained only the two trimarans, sailed by Crowhurst and Tetley. With the specter of Crowhurst catching up with him, or at least bettering his time for the cash prize, Nigel Tetley had pushed his trimaran hard. He had sailed almost entirely around the world, but his boat had become damaged, the structure joining the three hulls had weakened. In the middle of the night of May 21— 1,100 miles from England—his boat broke up and sank. Tetley took to his life raft and was picked up by a ship.

On June 29, in response to a BBC request for an ETA, Crowhurst radioed a Morse-code position of 32° north, 40° west (not far from where I am now, same latitude, several hundred miles due east). It was his last contact. Eleven days later, and about sixty miles farther north, the Royal Mail vessel *Picardy*, bound from London to the Caribbean, came across a ghosting trimaran. The ship sounded its foghorn three times. There was no response, so a boat was lowered and three of the *Picardy*'s crew boarded the trimaran. They found it as mysteriously deserted as the *Mary Celeste*. The life raft was still lashed on deck. Three blue logbooks lay on the chart table. The *Picardy* informed Lloyd's of London, which in turn notified the U.S. Air Force. A search was begun for a swimmer, or a body, but none was found. The *Picardy* hoisted the trimaran aboard and steamed on. A group from the *Sunday Times* flew to meet the *Picardy* when it docked in Santo Domingo, and the logbooks were handed over. They made stunning reading, revealing that Crowhurst had never left the Atlantic. They contained twenty-five thousand words of rambling mathematical and philosophical thoughts and revelations that showed a progressive decline into a madness brought on, in part, by a moral grief at what he had done. "It is finished, It is finished, IT IS THE MERCY," he had written in his final entry. It was deduced from his writings that at eleven-twenty A.M. on July 1, he had jumped into the sea and watched his trimaran sail on without him.

The news of Donald Crowhurst's deception, madness, and suicide was the lead story in most British newspapers on the weekend of July 27. The surviving competitors all wrote their books. Knox-Johnston's book, Moitessier's, and Tomalin and Hall's story of Crowhurst* are all still in print and selling well today, twenty-eight years after the end of the race.

Robin Knox-Johnston, the only finisher of the race, received both the Golden Globe and the £5,000 cash prize. He gave the money to the Crowhurst family.

I was unaware of all this at the time. I was no longer in England, where it is my habit to read the *Sunday Times*. I had returned to the United States. I was in college in Boston making my own chaotic voyages on LSD. I was protesting Vietnam. I had tuned in, turned on, and dropped out.

It was with one of my college tripping buddies that I planned to sell the Moroccan hashish Bill and I would sail across the Atlantic. When we sailed from Swansea (three years after the end of the Golden Globe Race) into our gale in the Bristol Channel, nothing in my life had prepared me for what was to come. In the middle of the first awful night, I sat huddled in the cockpit, on my watch, a small

*In the United States the title is *The Strange Last Voyage of Donald Crowhurst*.

transistor radio held to my ear benath my oilskin hood (before a wave doused me and put out the radio for good), listening to Beryl Reid, a British comedienne and actress, making a studio audience laugh. I wanted more than anything in the world to travel back through the ether to be among that audience blissfully unaware of the horror of being at sea on that night. Yet I couldn't get off the boat that night or in the foreseeable future because the weather made it unsafe for us to run for shore. I could not get off the boat at any price. That was the horror.

So I chose the only other way out: I got sicker. I escaped into a delirium of seasickness, leaving Bill to take care of everything. No wonder he finally called the lifeboat.

Jump a few years. I was writing advertising copy in London, had a little flat, had found what might in time have become a niche ashore. My one taste of sailing had terrified me, intrigued me, and left me with a funny, unidentifiable taste in my mouth. I went to the London Boat Show every January and read a few yachting magazines, but it went no further than that.

Then my parents, who had never sailed at all and must have gotten some notion about it from my misadventures, bought their *Viva III* and started preparing for their ill-fated third life. I went sailing with them on weekends and we learned the rudiments of sail-handling, anchoring, and navigation together. I noticed, on these cruises off England's south coast, even the rougher ones, that I did not get seasick.

One weekend morning, aboard *Viva* in the yachting port of Hamble, Hampshire, I woke up and saw *Suhaili* tied to the dock next to us. I recognized the boat immediately; I had found Knox-Johnston's book somewhere and read it twice, mesmerized, and pored over every detail of the rough, inelegant *Suhaili* in the color photographs. Robin Knox-Johnston was aboard, alone, puttering around on deck. He had stopped for the night, and before he took off again I said hello and talked to him for a while. *Suhaili* was unlike any yacht I had ever seen. She had a workboat finish: all paint—not a scrap of varnish to waste your time on—corrosion-mottled steel and iron fittings, some stained with rust. Yet she was beautiful, the way a tugboat can be beautiful. At thirty-two feet, she was twelve feet shorter than her neighbor *Viva*, but she had an outsize massiveness about her that made her appear to be a chunk hacked off a wooden whaling ship. I watched Knox-Johnston take *Suhaili* away from the dock with no more fuss than tying a shoelace, and motor off down the Hamble. I remember what I felt, watching him go: a massive sense of disparity between us, which, if I had been able to put into words, would have been: "There goes a man." And I was filled with an awareness of all that I was not, and had once, out in the Bristol Channel, so conspicuously failed to be.

In time, I came across the Crowhurst book, and Moitessier's. It became clear to me that alone at sea, in a dimension stripped of all possibility of pretense, the Golden Globe competitors had met their true selves—for better or worse—during the race. Moitessier had reached a spiritual plane that made the race seem pointless, made it impossible for him to turn left and sail to England for money or hollow acclaim. Crowhurst spent eight months inside a boat going nowhere, saturated with a deception that finally drove him to step off the deck into the water. And Knox-Johnston, despite damaging knockdowns from huge waves, and problems with his boat far worse than those which had demoralized and beaten other competitors, had learned that "I was thoroughly enjoying myself."

I read all three books again and again, and the funny taste in my mouth about my own aborted voyage grew bitter and shameful. I had experienced the tiniest inkling of what they had endured and I had curled up in my bunk and mewled and puked like a baby until I was rescued. I became aware of a sense of inadequacy that nothing, it seemed to me, but to go to sea alone someday would dispel. A gauntlet dropped in front of me and wouldn't go away. I wouldn't have to sail through the Southern Ocean and around the Horn, nor even around the world. To singlehand across an ocean would redeem me, would ease the disgrace I felt from that first trip to sea. . . .

This is too neat. I didn't think it all through like this. I believe now, looking back, this is part of what drove me subconsciously, kept me fascinated; but at the time, I was simply reading and rereading these three wildly different tales of the same event, thinking about singlehanding, and moving back toward boats after an initial episode that should have turned me off forever.

Certainly I didn't leave advertising to embark on a training scheme for eventual singlehanded sailing. I was trying to write a novel, and I quit my copywriting job because I felt I didn't have enough time for my own writing. But I was soon working on boats sailing around the Mediterranean, and not writing. Then J. and I got together, got married, and my thoughts of singlehanding took a backseat to the dream of the two of us following after the Hiscocks, doing that sybaritic circumnavigation by way of the Caribbean, Panama, the Pacific islands, New Zealand and Australia, the Indian Ocean, South Africa, and back up to the Caribbean. The Hiscock Highway, it has been dubbed. And after we had sailed together I couldn't imagine sailing without her.

But I am here at last. Not just sailing across the ocean to get to the other side, to Maine to sell the boat, as I originally set out to do; nor alone for lack of crew. I am sailing to meet my true self, and hoping to find an improved version. I don't want to see myself curling up again. I may have more than I bargained for, with the condition of my boat, but all I could have hoped for as a test. I must try to get *Toad* safely to land. I must be a man about it. I don't have to commit suicide and go down with the ship if it really sinks; I can try to save myself if the struggle ahead fails despite all my efforts.

But I must struggle well. That, finally, is what I'm here to do.

1800: Fixed the radio. It had to be the batteries. I tried one from another pack, substituting it one by one for the new ones—noise erupted. The sound is big, clear, and glorious! A bad battery! Second biggest scare of the voyage so far. Listening rather smugly to VOA's Jazz Hour now. Earlier, on the BBC, heard about the battle between the Royal Horticultural Society and a county cricket team over a British native orchid found growing on county cricket grounds. The horticulturists stopped play. Negotiations are scheduled. Without the radio I'd never have known.

Moving well. Pumping every hour, but life aboard is still good. This is still a wonderful trip. It's actually getting better and better.

July 24

Twenty-second day out of Horta.

We have been tearing along all night with the main slightly reefed, and at 0200 I go out on deck to roll the reef deeper. It is windier than an hour ago. Maybe because of the large dark rain cloud passing astern of us.

Below, I am unable to go back to sleep, feeling we are still over-canvased and hearing the sloshing in the bilges.

An hour later the cloud is gone and the wind is the same, about a steady twenty knots. I go forward and drop the genoa. I sit astride the bowsprit in the dark, bunching up the genoa and tying it to the whisker stays. I grip the four-inch-wide teak spar with my thighs like a bronco rider. My feet on the bobstay dip in and out of the warmish water as the bow rises and falls. I'm still not wearing a harness, not yet, it's not at all bad out. Just a lot different from what it has been for so long. And there is so much noise now: waves tumbling over themselves, and *Toad*'s insistent charging through them, and the steady cataract sound of the white water tumbling along both sides of the hull.

The boat is much happier under reefed main and staysail. Me too. I go below and fall asleep.

Still blowing this morning. Amazing difference from a few days ago. At noon we'll clock a good run at last. America is a thousand miles away but seems infinitely closer today. I feel it now just over the horizon. I picture it, New England in August: clams, lobsters, station wagons, sneakers and tattered sweatshirts; and toothsome American girls, strong, corn-fed, happy, impossibly normal. I imagine bringing *Toad* alongside some gray-bleached dock festooned with floats, stacked with lobster pots, and meeting one of these splendid, freckly girls. The ordinariness of it makes it seem so far beyond my reach. Is it real, or is it a J. Crew catalog?

At 0900 I notice a new sky. It is still blue and sunny, but high up there is now a lot of streaky cirrus.

> *If clouds appear as if scratched by a hen,*
> *Get ready to reef your topsails then.*

I get out Alan Watts's book and find this sky in Photograph 2: "Sky which means deterioration. The warm front of a depression is probably on its way . . . the wind will increase . . . rain is likely later."

The sea is up, too, after several days of this wind, confused and lumpy. A southerly swell now dominates over a steady procession of smaller waves from the northwest. *Toad* is being knocked about, slapped on the nose by the northwesterly lumps. But we are still making good progress, moving at five knots, heading northwesterly, straight for Maine.

However, Maine is still about 1,000 miles away. I have been thinking of making for Bermuda, now 400 miles due west. But with the wind up and from the southwest, I can't push *Toad* any closer to Bermuda than we're heading. When and if the wind shifts or drops, we will head that way.

A lot of water below, and more, always more, coming in. I pump now when I'm not doing anything else.

At local noon, 1330, my sights show we have made 112 miles in the last twenty-four hours. The log mileage is 121, so there is some current with the northwesterly swell which has set us back ten or eleven miles.

At 1500 and again at 1600, I roll up more of the main onto the boom. *Toad* is equipped with a roller-reefing gear that pulls the mainsail down and rolls it around the boom. Operated by a ratchet and pawl, it does its job quickly and neatly. I can roll up half the mainsail in about a minute. The remainder sets well on the mast, maintaining a taut, efficient airfoil shape. I can roll it down to stormsail size in two minutes. There is a photograph of this gear in

Hiscock's *Cruising Under Sail*. Turner's roller-reefing gear, it's called, manufactured in the 1930s. It works much faster than the modern system, laughably known as "jiffy" reefing, for its supposed speed of operation, which is what I found on all the new boats I've skippered or delivered.

Later in the afternoon I tune in to the shortwave weather forecast given by the U.S. Coast Guard station November Mike November in Portsmouth, Virginia, to see if they mention this weather. Two gales are moving east off the eastern seaboard, but that's way north, around 45° north.

And at 1800 I roll up still more of the main. The wind—I finally admit it—is much, much stronger now. It's blowing about thirty knots, a gale. We are being knocked and slammed about now. It is impossible to think of getting any closer to Bermuda at the moment. If I had thought of it days ago . . .

No matter how much I pump, water is now constantly sloshing over the floorboards. It has become wet and grimly depressing below. Gallons of water pouring without letup into an old boat bouncing around in the middle of the ocean without a proper life raft undermines your confidence, I find. I'm used to seeing an ocean of water outside, but a lot of it inside the boat where by essential principle it's supposed to be dry can get you down.

Just keep pumping. The Coast Guard forecast doesn't mention any weather system around here, so maybe it'll quiet down again soon. We'll go to Bermuda or maybe still poop on to Maine. It's hard to adjust to the fast-changing reality of life aboard: I keep thinking everything will be okay.

July 25

Haven't slept much. That sloshing noise. I worry about drifting off and letting too much water come in. When I do doze I dream we're sinking. Waking is hardly less nightmarish, with water above the floorboards.

The rain predicted by the Watts book comes in the night, with a low dark caving-in of cloud and those spatial hallucinations that make me feel we are turning and hobbyhorsing through great amorphous rooms. The strangest sensation, not unpleasant, but so strong tonight, probably because this is the lumpiest sea and weather of this voyage so far, and because I'm tired and it's easy, even a relief, to get carried away into it.

I have to watch myself. I know from all my book reading of sailors at sea and my own encounters with exhaustion that this is when you make mistakes. You let things go, let yourself and your boat down. I have to be vigilant. I have to eat to keep strong, and somehow I have to sleep. I have to sleep soon too, otherwise I risk getting so tired that when I wake up there will be too much water in the boat and I'll have lost the battle. Later this morning I'll nap.

We are converging with shipping lanes between northern Europe and ports in the Gulf of Mexico. We would never be seen by any lookout aboard a ship in such conditions. Nor would *Toad* be spotted on radar with all the wave clutter. And we've stopped moving now, so if I did see a ship looming up out of the murk, it would take long minutes to attempt evasive maneuvers. I'm relying on the statistical unlikelihood of collision, as John Letcher did for a while. We are hove-to, staysail backed and the reefed main sheeted flat amidships, bobbing quite comfortably, pointing west, probably making a knot of leeway to the northwest, which is where we want to go. I want to see if heaving-to, reducing our motion, slows the water coming in. Can't tell yet. It's four o'clock in the morning.

Under way again at 0800. Tried napping, and maybe dozed a little but not much. Just as much water coming in, so we might as well keep going and we're making good time in the right direction. The wind is still a steady twenty-eight to thirty knots.

A lot of water, in fact, is coming in. More than yesterday. It is unhinging to have this much water coming in and no visible hole in the boat. I pump all the time now when I'm not doing anything else vital. Sleep is vital, but I can't seem to manage it. The floor is continually underwater now. I wade through the interior of the boat. Yet I seem to be able to keep it around that level.

Local noon is 1335, and I'm lucky enough to get a sight of the sun for latitude. Earlier this morning I managed two quick snapshots of a hazy but sufficiently distinct orb through cloud. We're at 35°18' north, 52°45' west. Eighty-three miles since noon yesterday, which is good for being hove-to and slowed down. This boat sails well.

Marking my penciled X on the chart, I find we are again at one of those spots on the ocean where I've been before. Two years ago, on July 16, J. and I were just three miles away with the cats aboard *Toad*, bound for the Azores. A year ago, on June 28, we were five miles away on *Sea Bear*, a boat we delivered from Florida to England.

Sea Bear was a Moody 33, a modern plastic boat designed by Angus Primrose, the English yacht designer who had the great misfortune to go to sea in one of his own boats—something designers rarely do—a Moody 33 called *Demon Demo*. Primrose sailed it across the Atlantic in the OSTAR (the London *Observer* Single-handed Trans-Atlantic Race), during which, in not particularly severe weather, *Demon Demo* was rolled upside down, losing its rig. Primrose was sailing the boat off the U.S. east coast several years later, supposedly alone, while Mrs. Primrose remained in England, when again *Demon Demo* capsized during a gale. This was a bad Gulf Stream storm, a northerly gale blowing against the north-setting current creating dangerous seas. J. and I were coming down the

Chesapeake from Annapolis in a new bareboat, to deliver offshore to the Virgin Islands, when this same storm brewed up. We were lucky enough to hear about its approach on the radio and sat it out in Little Creek Harbor at the mouth of the Chesapeake. Offshore, a number of boats got into trouble, and when *Demon Demo* capsized, Primrose, who was not in fact alone, but with a young lady, launched the life raft and got his passenger into it. She later said that before he had a chance to follow her, another wave broke over the boat and down it went, taking its creator.

Sea Bear was ugly and uncomfortable, though fast, and we were luckier than its designer with the weather. At one point we spent five days and nights flying a large spinnaker and traveling at its maximum hull speed of between six and seven knots through dense fog south of the Grand Banks, frightened to death of meeting a ship or an errant iceberg, but knowing there was not much difference between slow and fast in such a situation.

This afternoon we're being knocked about too much, and tons of water are filling the boat, so I heave-to again, feeling, for the first time, a little desperate, unsure if I am able to handle what's happening. I want to keep moving, get closer to Bermuda, but moving seems to make the leak worse—although, finally, it's hard to tell. My attitude is changing fast. For a while, around teatime, that English ritual so suggestive of warmth and coziness that I observe most days at sea, I lose my nerve and think of putting out a mayday call. It's not warm and cozy at all aboard the boat now, but wet and loud and fucking terrifying.

Never mind, then, have a nice cup of tea.

" 'Ere, 'ave a nice cuppa tea, luv," I say aloud in my best Eastender charlady accent. " 'At's right, put the kettle on. Lovely! An' a bit of that bread—why don't you toast it, luv? You got this bleedin' oven wiv a grill, use it! Go on! Give yourself a lit'le treat, then. All you bin froo. Yes, lovely! An' a bit of that jam. A proper tea! 'At's it!"

Whoever she is, she's wonderful. She makes me a lovely tea. And keeps cooing "Love-lee!" as she does it. I'll hang on to her for a bit.

I should sleep. I'm tired—you're exhausted, you've *got to sleep*—but I'm afraid to let myself go all the way, because I don't know at what point, if I stop to sleep, the water coming in will become too much ever to get ahead of again. If x amount is coming in now and I can keep ahead of it, can I pump out enough water after y minutes of sleep? I don't know the answer, and I'm too terrified to get it wrong. And behind that is the fear that once asleep I simply won't hear the alarm.

This evening I do a marathon stint at the pump, getting glimpses of solid floorboard for a few minutes. Then I turn on the radio and hear McCoy Tyner on the Jazz Hour. I make spaghetti.

I eat my bowl of spaghetti sitting on the saloon bunk with my feet up out of the water on a towel in front of me. Looking around the cabin, I'm intensely glad J. isn't here tonight to see this water sloshing over the floor, to see *Toad* reduced to this. To fear for it now as I do. We had more good times than bad aboard this boat, I still think. Most of all when we pulled up the anchor and sailed somewhere. We worked in concert, and felt our boat respond. Once we had fixed it up, the vision we shared of a sailing life seemed, for a short while, to come true. Our three-month cruise from the Virgin Islands to Florida by way of Puerto Rico, the Dominican Republic, and the Bahamas was the nearest we came to reaching paradise together.

It takes time to become part of a place, especially in a pit stop for transients, and after nearly three years of floating around St. Thomas and St. John, just as we were about to leave, we seemed finally to have arrived. People knew us and our rugged little boat. Ed Dwyer, who ran Water Island Charters and had given us so much work and become a friend, offered all the charters both of us might want and deliveries of new boats from the east coast down to the

Virgins. Dieter, the German blacksmith, asked us to run his sixty-five-footer for its first charter season. We said no, thank you, pleased at the recognition, but we'd had it with the Virgins. It had been mostly heartbreak and effort. We were already gone.

Two days before we sailed away, we got another kitty from the Humane Society, a black skinny thing with huge ears. Ed Dwyer said he looked like a bat. We called him Neptune. He was to be a friend for Minou, who pummeled him and ignored him before he finally fell in love. But it was me Neptune chose to favor. After two days of hiding aboard, he appeared on my chest one morning and began rubbing his nose against my whiskery chin, purring like an outboard. He became "my boy" and I loved him more than Minou.

We sailed first to San Juan, Puerto Rico, where we met an American sailor, Rick, and his Spanish girlfriend, Cruz, whom he had picked up in the Canary Islands while crossing the Atlantic. His boat was a nice, rather run-down old wooden double-ender; but what made it noticeable was the thing that looked like an umbrella without any fabric open and lashed to the top of the mast. It was a lightning protection device, he said. He had already been struck twice ("¡Aïe!" said Cruz, remembering) and designed his umbrella, after consulting numerous books, to ward off future attacks. Two years later when we were passing through Horta, in the Azores, Bob Silverman (whose house and lifestyle there I admired) gave us more news of Rick and his wonderful bad luck. Approaching Fayal the year before, Rick had taken a nap, the wind had changed, and his wind vane-steered, umbrella-protected boat had piled into the foot of a cliff at the west end of the island. Rick and Cruz, wearing only shorts and T-shirts, jumped onto the rocks as the boat sank beneath them and spent the entire night scaling a steep cliff until they were crawling through the hydrangea bushes on level land at dawn. They were found bloody, shocked, insensible, and brought to the local hospital. When they recovered, they were given a ride on to England aboard another yacht. As that yacht entered the English Channel it was run down and sunk by a French trawler. Rick and

Cruz were both injured, but made it ashore to England alive. I don't know if they went sailing again, but I'd bet anything he did. He had too much bad luck going for him to leave it at that. People like that are persistent, and lucky too in a funny way, because they always survive, despite any amount of wreckage and dead or injured people they leave in their wake. Rick is still out there, sailing toward a fresh disaster, with a really unlucky, unsuspecting companion unaware of what's about to happen.

From Puerto Rico we sailed on through fabled waters. La Isla Española, Columbus named the large, lush, high island he found to the south of his first landfall, in honor of his Spanish patrons. Hispaniola it became, and still is, shared by the states of Haiti and the Dominican Republic. On the quiet Christmas night of 1492, the *Santa Maria* grounded on a coral reef off the north coast, near what is now Cap Haiten. It stuck fast and was abandoned, leaving its Spanish timbers to rot in the New World. On this bloody island sugar plantations worked by Carib and Arawak Indian slaves were the first planted endeavor of the colonial aspirations from across the Atlantic.

We stopped at several ports in the Dominican Republic. Samaná, described in our guidebook as a picturesque village on the east coast, had recently been razed and rebuilt by the government in readiness for a hoped-for onslaught of tourism. It had rows of project-looking concrete buildings in which the dispossessed people of Samaná now lived like glum squatters, empty concrete hotels, and wide concrete roads leading nowhere.

It took us four days to sail the ninety-odd miles from Puerta Plata, on the Dominican Republic's north coast, to Great Inagua, the southernmost island of the Bahamas. We got about halfway there and the wind died and we lay becalmed. We sat under the awning and ate the incredible-tasting avocados and pineapples we had bought in Puerta Plata. ("How much are the avocados?" "Sixty cents a dozen." *"What?"* *"Bueno,* forty cents.") We read. And we listened to the Voice of America tracking Skylab as, unplanned, the space station fell out of its orbit and began hurtling earthward at so shallow an angle that NASA wasn't really sure where it was going to crash onto the planet's surface. Most of the earth's surface, the VOA announcers pointed out reassuringly, was covered with water, so people on land shouldn't worry. And much of the eighty-ton, eighty-two-foot-long Skylab would burn up in the long oblique plunge through the atmosphere, so what did reach that remote spot of water somewhere would simply be a few tons of white-hot flaming debris. The coverage, as the fiery descent began, made it all sound like a sporting event, the commentators excitedly reporting that now it was over the Bering Sea, dropping fast, then streaking southeast across the Canadian tundra, now over open ocean, hurtling down the Atlantic; it was anybody's guess where it would land; NASA's latest estimates were being revised; it's got to be starting to burn up about now—

I looked up, scanning the sky to the north for what would at first appear as fireworks but then very quickly grow infinitely bigger, imagining that we might actually be unluckier than Rick and Cruz and have a space station drop on us. It seemed worse not having an engine, not having the option of cranking it up and then, once the fiery comet of debris was sighted, being able to steam out of its way at five knots.

However, it wasn't even a close call. Skylab scattered itself over the eastern Indian Ocean and western Australia, hopefully not disturbing even so much as a wallaby, or any Aussie yachties.

The Bahamian islands stretching south and east from Nassau, the capital, on New Providence Island—the Exuma Cays, Cat Island, Long Island, San Salvador (generally agreed to be Columbus's first landfall in the New World), Crooked and Acklins, Mayaguana, and Great and Little Inagua—are known to the Bahamians as the Out Islands. Perhaps because they are really *out there*. They lie north of eastern Cuba. They offer no facilities to the visitor, and the world largely passes them by. To me they felt as remote from the rest of the world as any place I've ever been.

We were sailing in the wake of one of my sailing heroes. In the sixties, Eric and Susan Hiscock sailed *Wanderer III* across the Atlantic to the Caribbean, the Bahamas, and the U.S. east coast. *Toad* followed *Wanderer*'s path through the Out Islands and we stopped at many of the anchorages mentioned in Eric's book *Atlantic Cruise in Wanderer III*: French Wells, Calabash Bay, Big Major's Spot. In these places I took photographs of *Toad*, riding to anchor just where *Wanderer* had, copying Eric's plates in the book as closely I could. I even surreptitiously lured J. to spots on the sand where Susan had stood, where the composition was a perfect match, and then pressed the shutter. J. would admonish me, telling me to focus on our trip, not the Hiscocks', but it gave me a little thrill.

The Bahamas lie at the edge of the Great Bahama Bank, a plateau of sand almost five hundred miles long, which separates the islands from Cuba. The average depth is fifteen feet, and often in the atmosphere over the bank miles ahead, you can see "bank blink," a pale green reflection of the shallow water below. On the other side of the islands, in places only several hundred yards from the bank, is the Atlantic Ocean, with depths plunging quickly to fifteen thousand feet. In the cuts between the islands, where these waters meet, tidal currents are strong—far stronger than *Toad*'s sail-powered ability to breast them. We had to play the tides like sailors of old. Navigation was all "eyeball": gauging depths and bottom type by the color of the water and the state of the tide by a glance ashore as we shot through cuts and ran, tacked, jibed, and beat through an endless maze of tiny islands and labyrinthine coral reefs, around great mushroom-shaped coral heads that sprouted from the sandy bottom with only a dark patch to warn of their position. Our passage up through the Out Islands was our final exam in handling a small boat under sail. We had heard the scuttlebutt about the Bahamas: it was a tricky place and many boats were lost there. But we did fine.

The Out Islands seemed deserted that summer. In our first month there, we saw only one other yacht, a singlehander on a tiny boat heading south. The Out Islands even had their own lonely sound, which we always heard when we stepped ashore from the dinghy: a soughing made by the trade wind through the casuarina pines that grew with the sea grape along the shore. It reminded us both of the wind in the pines in Mallorca when we were children.

In three months we spent $100 on vegetables, limes, and ice cream bought at tiny shack stores in Out Island villages, and on cold beer when we hove in sight of a bar. We carried no beer aboard because we had no refrigeration and didn't like it warm. At the end of every day, anchored in quiet water watching the brief and always beautiful tropical twilight, we drank glasses filled with rum, crushed limes, water, and a little sugar. During the day we drank gallons of water, of which we always had plenty because we caught it from passing squalls in our cockpit awning, which emptied through a small tube straight into our tanks. We dove every day for grouper, crayfish, or conch, for us and "the boys." I used a Hawaiian sling rather than a speargun: a slingshot made of surgical rubber bound to the side of a hollow wooden handle. The spear goes through the handle and is pulled back and released. You had to get close to your quarry, and then pull and fire. We saw shark and barracuda but we didn't bother them and they didn't bother us. We ate well on whatever I speared four or five nights a week with rice or vegetables, and spaghetti or rice on nights when we were glutted on fish or crayfish—the southern lobster. We found wild papaya and coconuts. We baked bread. We grew as brown and fit as savages from swimming and diving for our food and hauling up the anchor and raising sails and winching sheets and walking entirely around every island we anchored at.

This was J. and I at our best, working our boat together, feeding ourselves, exploring each passing island and moving on. We felt we could have lived like this indefinitely, we dallied and zigzagged, but we were moving inexorably closer to the States and the end of our cruise.

In the Berry Islands, north of Nassau, we sheltered in a land-locked bay as Hurricane David roared up through the Bahamas and passed sixty miles south of our hurricane "hole." The roof of a solitary house ashore behind us blew off, but our anchors—three of them, triangulated for a hold against any change of wind direction—held firmly, and we weathered the blow looking out our portholes at the spume-filled air, and listening to Florida radio stations a hundred miles away that tracked the storm. The local Bahamian station had switched, near the height of the storm, to a live, endless, imploring church service as a means of ultimate storm protection for its listeners. When the hurricane had passed, we found crayfish, disoriented by churned-up sand and strange currents, walking drunkenly along open sandy stretches of bottom, out of their usual holes in the coral, and we picked up eight of them in five minutes and ate them all the way to Fort Lauderdale.

We spent six months in Fort Lauderdale, and another year anchored off Dinner Key south of Miami. A dispiriting time when we tried to make enough money to sail away, but there was never enough, or as much as we thought we would need. I hadn't yet read Sterling Hayden's autobiography *Wanderer* (Hayden was a sailing ship master before he became what he called a male starlet), in which he writes: "To be truly challenging, a voyage, like a life, must rest on a firm foundation of financial unrest. Otherwise you are doomed to a routine traverse." We did some delivery work: sailing new boats from Florida and Annapolis to the Virgins for charter companies, a ten- to twelve-day trip, usually an unpleasant beat to windward all the way, in crappy boats not designed or prepared to go to sea but for a doodle around the gentle Virgins. I bought a good sextant in a varnished wooden box from Sy Carkhuff, who had sailed around the world with it, and my sun and star sights improved on these offshore passages. I also worked as a boat carpenter around Dinner Key, and J. did some boat painting and varnishing.

We plunged back into our old malaise. We fought more often and more unkindly. A constant dull unhappiness grew between us by the steady accretion of little episodes. The same way a coral reef is built.

After eighteen months we decided to leave again. Rather the way we'd felt when we left the Virgins: it was time to flee. We knew we didn't have enough money to get as far as New Zealand, a year's voyage with no possibility of making money on the way, so we headed east across the Atlantic.

This voyage was not the happy uninterrupted dream sequence of our Out Islands cruise. We sailed out of No Name Harbor on Key Biscayne, into the Gulf Stream a couple of miles offshore, where the wind died and we were swept away north in the five-knot current. That first evening we had a terrible fight, shouting at each other. I remember the shouting but not what it was about, but it's never about what sets it off. The weather remained light all the way to Bermuda, and it took us fifteen days to get there.

After two weeks in Bermuda, the bilges filled with water the day we left, frightening us, but we discovered it had been coming in through the unsecured forward hatch—and then it stopped. The Azores, three weeks out. A month on Fayal. Then a week to the European mainland, rounding Cape St. Vincent on a sunny after-noon and Portugal looked so pretty, but we were screaming at each other. *"I'm sick of you! I'm sick to death of you!"* I remember yelling at J., hoarsely, and her yelling it back.

We almost put the boat ashore just north of Tarifa at the entrance to the Straits of Gibraltar. We had tacked in toward the land all night seeking a lee against the tremendous blast of a *levante,* an easterly gale blowing out of the straits. Tack after tack after tack, exhausting ourselves, we became drenched and cold inside our oil-skins, and a dulling numbness came over us. In the misty dawn we saw ahead the lights of cars on the coast road shown on our chart, but we didn't see that this was well inland from the beach. Before we were aware of it in our blunted state, we were in the waves off the beach. We had expected the water to flatten out as we approached the shore, with the gale blowing off the land, but so great was the force of the wind that they were still high and breaking only yards from dry sand. We let the sheets fly, the sails flap, and I jumped straight into the water off the bow and stood hip deep and pushed *Toad*'s bow off into deeper water. A day later we ghosted into Gibraltar, the northern Pillar of Hercules, and the remarkable juxtaposition of a hideous English suburban town on the shores of the Mediterranean.

Our final break came not with a bang but a series of whimpers. We left *Toad* in Ibiza, one island short of our destination of Mallorca because we could bear to sail no farther together. I left almost immediately for London. J. followed two months later, after she had found a home for the cats with someone in Germany because there was no bringing them to England with a six-month-long quarantine. That must have destroyed her, giving them away; that and the abandonment of our home for a studio I was renting from my mother. We spent an unhappy winter and spring together in London. I was trying to write again, after years of thinking but doing nothing about it. J. hated sharing me again, particularly with the people we saw in London, whom she found to be superficial. She hated the way she felt about herself around me. That summer we got the job delivering *Sea Bear* from Florida to England. In the early fall we sailed *Toad* from Ibiza to England. Our final passage together. Martin came with us as far as Motril on the Spanish mainland, where we met Whit, who so disapproved of scrimshaw, and J. and I had one more fight. She left Martin and me in a bar there one night and when I got back to the boat I found a note from her: "I know when I'm like this I'm my own worst enemy, making you want to abandon me."

We spent two weeks at sea being quiet and careful with each other. We made love for the last time. We got pummeled by the equinoctial gales off the Western Approaches to the Channel. We left *Toad* at its winter berth off Flushing and listed it with a local yacht broker.

One day, back in London, after food-shopping by myself in

Waitrose on the King's Road, I went home and told J. I couldn't live with her anymore. I did this instinctually, appalled at myself, in the face of my love for her and my feeling that she was the best person I knew or might ever know and my vision of what we could have been together. None of that seemed to help. I was exhausted with trying to make her happy, sick of seeing myself at my worst through her eyes, and seeing her at her worst, frightened of the way we fought like two alpha wolves trapped in a cage, wounding each other and going for those same raw wounds the next time.

She had expected it all along—almost from the day of our wedding, I realize now. It came as proof of the inerasable lesson she had learned as a nine-year-old girl on vacation with her parents when one day her mother vanished with the handsome tennis pro: the people you love will leave you.

She didn't fight me; she didn't say, *Let's work this out.* She took what I said as absolute as a papal decree and boarded a train to Nice to stay with her mother. She saw the Bergstroms again, and Leif asked her if she wanted to be part of a crew with him delivering a motor yacht to Florida. She went, about six weeks after we split, and they are still together.

I have thought, since leaving her, that we might have been perfect together if we could have met for the first time as the people we were when we split up—or perhaps quite a bit later. People who had acquired some knowledge of marital relations and could use it to make one work. Or if we had stayed together and rebuilt our relationship as we had rebuilt *Toad*, cutting out the rot back to what was clean and sound, and building on the good stuff. But I didn't see how we could do that any more than meet each other again for the first time.

I started running. I got up early every morning and ran through the dark around Bishop's Park in Fulham, beside the Thames. I ran longer and longer distances. Across Putney bridge and down the towpath along the river to Hammersmith. Five miles, then ten miles. It seemed the only thing in the world I could do that did something in return for me. The longer I ran, the better I felt.

I went on the dole (I gave my occupation as boat captain, and, there not being any such jobs at that time in Fulham, I was given £90 a week).

I ran the London marathon in March.

I spent most of my time in my little studio, writing, and reading boating books, magazines, and taking my sextant out of its varnished box and looking at it. I felt marooned. David and Martin were well embarked on their careers, but not in positions from which they could help me get in. I found my old portfolio of ads and thought of trying to get back into advertising. I wrote and drew new spec ads. I wrote one for Seiko watches, about how Peter Nichols used his to navigate across the Atlantic. But it was a bad time to try to get back in, I was told.

I wondered what I was doing, and who I was, alone, in my thirties, now, living at home with my mother, broke and on the dole. Such thoughts flew at me like van Gogh's dark crows between two and four o'clock in the morning, and I had no answers.

Increasingly I thought of *Toad*. Unsold, waiting. I thought of sailing it somewhere by myself. I felt capable of this now; I knew this would make me feel better about myself.

Finally, it was all I could think of.

July 26

Spend most of the day in the cockpit. In my foul-weather gear, my harness on now because I'm getting some sleep, sitting upright over the pump, back against the cabin, nodding off between strokes. Rocked and bounced to sleep. Getting real sleep too, must be, because I'm dreaming vividly. Dreamed we were approaching the Azores. Woke up once and saw Maine ahead, for sure, all those granite shores and fir trees. Straight out of *WoodenBoat* magazine. Eggemoggin Reach, I guessed. Thought about getting up and going forward to unlash the anchor and then it wasn't there and I realized we still had about eight hundred miles to go. A lot of dreams like that all day.

Hove-to. No sailing. Boat full of water, although I can go below and wade around pretty easily.

I put the battery (a Die Hard car battery, which powers my tape deck and VHF radio) into the cooler, which is floating where the engine would be. I have to keep it dry, keep the VHF working.

No sun today, so no position. No one makes me tea either. Not that sort of day. Or else she's on holiday.

Odd, but there's this white stuff in the water today, all around the boat, particularly as we roll in the swell. Little white bits, like chunks of barnacle you scrape off the hull when you haul out, only a little smaller. In the water around the boat. Waves cleaning the hull? The stuff sinks slowly. I watch it go down. Bits of something.

I think it's windier today, if anything. A real gale, over thirty knots. The seas are up from yesterday—but they would be, after days of this.

Might try the radio later, put out a call, see if anyone's there.

An endless night, pumping when I'm not dozing. Pump-pump-pump. Back and forth, back and forth, a rhythm building, like prostration for prayer. It's cloudy, but through the cloud comes the dim illumination from a new moon somewhere above, giving the night shape and texture: gloomy rooms with inchoate frescoed ceilings, dark, heaving walls.

July 27

At dawn I see a ship off to the north, four or five miles away. Very hazy, dawn light and misty air, but it stays there and keeps going like a real ship while I stand up and watch it.

I go below and call it up on the VHF.

"Hello ship at about 35°43' north, 53°03' west, this is the sailing yacht *Toad* several miles off your port beam. Do you read? Over."

An answer, from a Dutch ship. He claims it's not him I see because he doesn't see me anywhere off his port beam, or on radar. He tells me I'm probably seeing another ship. I don't care. I have rehearsed what I want to say.

"I am in a severely leaking condition. I am en route to Bermuda. I may have to abandon ship. Would you please radio the U.S. Coast Guard station November Mike November and let them know my position and situation, and ask them to alert shipping in this area to keep a good lookout in case I have to abandon ship?"

The Dutch ship will have a shortwave transmitter. My VHF will transmit no farther usually than you can see from its aerial at the top of the mast: maybe twenty miles, possibly farther at sea in good conditions.

"You need to get off now?"

I'm not prepared for this question.

"*Jacht*, you want to abandon ship now?"

"No, thanks. I'm hoping to make it to Bermuda. But my boat is leaking, and I may have to abandon ship later."

"*Ja*, okay."

I wait a little while, then call back to see if he got through, but I get no answer. I call several more times without a response. I go back on deck and look to the northwest, but the ship is gone. It's still blowing about thirty knots.

Immediately, I start thinking I should have said, "Yes, I'm sinking. I have to get off now. Please save me."

What constitutes sinking? I wonder. Is *Toad* sinking? Even now, this is almost a new concept. It has a leak, but is it *sinking*? How bad is it? How accustomed to it have I become?

What if I don't see another ship?

When do I let go?

I pump for a long time, but there is still water over the floor below. I go down to find something to eat. No bread left. There is some muesli. I haven't made a proper meal for several days. Spaghetti, when was that? I look in the lockers around the galley, not really seeing what I'm looking at. Didn't I have some peanut butter?

I drift, standing in the galley, holding on while the boat lurches back and forth, my mind blank.

"Hello, *Toad*!" An incredibly cheery voice on the radio, which I've left on. "Little boat *Toad*!" An Indian accent. "Hello! Hello! Hello!"

I pick up the mike. "Yes, hello. This is *Toad*."

"*Toad*, yes! Good morning! How are you?"

How am I? "I am leaking, thank you. How are you?"

"Oh, yes, you are leaking!" A definite chuckle. "That is what we are hearing! But we are fine, thank you! Very good, very good!"

The Indian accent, beloved of comics and mimics in England, is thick, and irrepressibly cheerful. It sounds like Peter Sellers, escaped from *The Party* and running amok on the high sea. If I were anywhere else—hearing this on the phone, say—I would know it was a joke.

And even here I say, "Who is this?"

"We are the ship *Laxmi*. We are calling to see if you need help. How are you, really?"

"Where are you?"

"We are here!"

We are here is not a position a professional seaman would be likely to give. The sense of joke compounds, turns surreal.

"I mean what is your position, please?"

"But we are right here, *Toad*! Look! Look out the door, please!"

Still holding the mike, I step up on the galley counter and look out—

A ship is *right* behind us, on top of us. I could whack a bad-minton birdie onto its deck. Big, black, rusty, a cargo ship of some sort. LAXMI written on its bow. The bridge towers overhead, and eight or ten grinning Indians are crowding the rail above my head, waving as if I were Prince Charles. I can hear them shouting: "Hello, *Toad*!" I wave back.

"You see!" says the laughing voice on the radio. "We are here!"

"Yes, I see," I answer back into the mike.

We all wave for a while.

"Well, do you want to come with us?"

That question again. Get off or wait? For what? It's still blowing. I'm not doing well. I'm tired and dopey. And I don't think the leak is going to slow down when the wind drops. I've reached a crossroad.

"Where are you going?" I ask.

"We are going to Burma!"

"Burma?"

"Yes, Burma! You know, next door to India!"

What a thought! What might be waiting for me in Burma? Perhaps I could turn into a Somerset Maugham character, become an old Burma "hand." Manage a rubber plantation, wear baggy shorts and a pith helmet, and start drinking a lot of gin. Trim my mustache to an RAF shape and marry the daughter of a missionary, Celia, with whom I would have brittle fights on the veranda after dinner. Go quietly mad. Or perhaps go native—"poor chap, bad business"—and meet a Burmese woman and raise a bunch of beau-tiful Eurasian children. Or become a Buddhist monk. Or would I find my appointment in Samarra, the death I had unknowingly been headed toward all along? I think of these old clichés and realize I know nothing at all about the modern Burma. All the more reason to go.*

Here at the crossroad, *Laxmi* is unmistakably the less-traveled road, forking toward Burma. And, with some disappointment in myself, I fail to rise to the occasion.

"No, thanks, *Laxmi*. I'm trying to get to the States. Or Bermuda."

"You are sure?"

"Yes, thanks." And now I'll always wonder.

I ask *Laxmi* to radio the Coast Guard at NMN in Portsmouth, Virginia, to tell them about me and my situation. They promise to do this and, with lots of waving and wide white smiles, they steam off to the southeast.

Will this be the last ship I see? I'm sure not. It's the second I've seen in an hour. We must be bang in the middle of the shipping lane.

A little later *Laxmi* calls back. They're in touch with the Coast Guard, who are asking for an ETA in Maine or Bermuda. Eight to ten days, or three or four for Bermuda, I tell my pal aboard *Laxmi*. In our last exchange, he gives me a position check, which puts me considerably farther to the northeast than where I think I am. One of us is about forty miles off.

The sun appears at 1030 and I get two LOP snapshots. I work them out and find that I am, in fact, where I thought I was. I believe in my navigation, and wonder whether *Laxmi* will make Burma after all.

With the sun comes a sudden dramatic moderation of wind and weather. By noon it's a nice day, blowing about twelve knots. The sea is still lumpy, but it's time to crack on more sail, which will steady us and get us moving. I'm invigorated. I feel wide awake.

I go up on deck and unroll all of the main. Then I go out on the bowsprit, sit down on it, and start untying the genoa.

*Since this voyage, I have learned something of Aung San Suu Kyi and the troubles of modern Burma.

My feet and legs and the bobstay chain are plunging in and out of the water as *Toad* rises and falls in the leftover swell. At the lower edge of my vision I suddenly register a large dark shape in the water immediately beneath my feet. I'm back on deck, well inboard, saying out loud "Je-sus *Christ!*" before I know it. It was huge, dark brown, and bobbing at my feet with a curious undulating motion, as if sniffing me.

I lean over the edge of the deck and look down. My God, what is that? The weirdest creature I've ever seen, huge too: flat, ragged, torn, waving in the water—

It's the sheathing. Delaminated from the bow, hanging off the hull in a long wide flap of heavy cloth, brown with dried resorcinol glue, waving up and down in the water with the motion of the waves. I move out onto the bowsprit again to get a better look and see the same waving flap down the other side of the boat too. The Cascover has delaminated at its joint at the bow and peeled back down both sides of the boat, at least halfway back, as far as I can see. Great obscene flaps waving from amidships. How long has it been like this?

I see those white bits in the water again, and now I know exactly what they are: old caulking, dried and brittle, washing out of the seams.

Dizzy, with a cold feeling in my stomach, I rush below and look at the hull up forward. Plain as day, seawater is pouring in, welling arterially, through most seams, as far back as the saloon, and farther. White bits of old caulking have also been pushed in and are lying on the planking and down the sides of the frames. Everywhere. Haven't I seen this until now? Known, without looking overboard, how bad it was? I don't know. If I saw it, I pushed away its meaning.

I don't know if I've been holding my breath, but now I can't breathe. I rush topside again.

I sit in the cockpit. I'm feeling dizzy. Hard to breathe. I sit, holding on. Minutes pass.

The boat, I realize—I knew it all along—is quite sound. All those sister frames, and the new laminated floor frames I put in just two years ago before we left Florida. The boat is as strong as ever. But the sheathing is off, the caulking gone or going from half the seams in the hull's planking. The boat has turned into a colander.

Nothing I can do about it . . . is there? A hole I could patch: I could saw up the plywood beneath the bunks and nail it over ten holes. But this . . . I think of Robin Knox-Johnston caulking *Suhaili*'s leaking seam underwater with a complicated patch. Eight feet of seam on both sides of the boat. What would he do here with the equivalent of forty fifteen-foot-long kerfs sawn through the hull? And certain to lengthen.

Toad is gone. I know this absolutely as I sit here in the cockpit on what is now becoming rather a nice day. The sun is out, the sea is going down.

Knowing this, I look at the boat around me. The teak vent boxes I built on the cabin roof. The stainless steel guardrail stanchions I installed. The winches, the rigging. The new compass Martin and I hooked up. The slight imperfection beneath the paint on the cabin side that I know is my plug of a hole made by Henry's useless depth gauge. I look up and down the boat and I cannot see an inch of it that I haven't remade according to my idea of what would make *Toad* the best it could be. Now I know that the leak will not get better but worse, that I can't keep ahead of it, that I must get off, save my life, and let *Toad* sink.

I have never thought of *Toad* as "she," the way many think of their boats. My brother David liked to call it "him." To me *Toad* doesn't have a gender, but it is certainly something far more than the sum of its wood and bits and pieces. With every screw and bolt and pass of a paintbrush that J. and I gave it, this boat made these its own, and added something of itself. It has absorbed more love into its fibers than any amount of paint or varnish, until this has become part of its matrix. What *Toad* is to me now is a thing that was made and lives from that love.

And I believe *Toad* loves me back.

So as I sit in the cockpit and look at it with tears pouring down my face, I am careful to keep quiet. I don't say anything. I'm not going to tell it what is going to happen now.

I sheet the main amidships, heaving-to, and wait for local noon. I get a latitude sight. I work out our position with unusual care, thinking about our drift since the morning LOP sights. We're at 36°08′ north, 53°12′ west. Three hundred miles northeast of Bermuda; eight hundred miles from Maine.

At 1400 I put out my first mayday call on the VHF. I say into the mike, according to international radio etiquette: "Mayday, mayday, mayday. This is the sailing yacht *Toad* at 36°08′ north, 53°12′ west, requesting assistance. Mayday, mayday, mayday. This is the sailing yacht *Toad* at 36°08′ north, 53°12′ west, requesting assistance."

No reply. I repeat it a few more times, then stop. I haven't been heard. Probably no ship within range. I'll wait an hour and try again. I'll do this every hour on the hour, but for no more than two or three minutes, to conserve battery power. I know this part of the ocean, I know this is a shipping lane. I've spoken with two ships already this morning. Another will come along. I cling positively to this thought so I don't have to think about getting into the dinghy and sailing for Bermuda. I think instead of what to take when a ship comes along and takes me off. I start to pack.

This is a good time to go through my wardrobe and get rid of a few things. At this singular moment in my life, an article comes to mind, written by Michael Korda some time ago in *The New York Times Magazine*. It was on the subject of a man's irreducible minimum wardrobe. A man can make do, Korda wrote, with one suit and two shirts. He can wash the shirts in a basin at night, hanging them up to dry, and if the suit is made of a decent wool, he can hang it in the bathroom when he takes his shower, and the steam will remove any wrinkles. I wondered, when I read this, how Korda, scion of the family of cinema titans, who grew up surrounded by wealth and abundance, who has himself become a famous editor in

chief of a publishing house and best-selling author, came by such knowledge, which would indicate both impoverishment and a great concern to maintain appearances, and why he would write about this during the prime of his own adult success. These tactics and concern might have come from his uncle, Alexander Korda, a penniless Hungarian refugee who made himself into a movie tycoon and married Merle Oberon. I suppose the fear of loss of newly gained wealth, and how to manage without it, and regain it, is carried subconsciously down through several generations. It might have been something Michael Korda learned at the knee of his illustrious uncle, essential information that any man must carry to make his way in the world, and that, I guessed, is why Korda was moved to write the article and pass it on.

Anyway, I think of it now as I go through my own clothes. I don't have a suit, but I do have a blazer, wool, and I stuff it into a sailbag. I'll pull it out when I have my next shower. I have a number of shirts, out of which I select two Brooks Brothers button-downs, and several T-shirts. A pair of venerable jeans. Underwear, socks, a hankie Martin gave me. I hope this will do. I have no idea what this next boatless phase in my life will bring, or what I will have to become in it, or how often I will have to shower with my blazer.

I look around at my books. Hundreds of them stuffed into the shelves above the saloon berths, over the chart table, in the back of the galley. Years of selecting and collecting. Mostly they are books about boats and the sea. How to design them, build them, sail them. By the designers, builders, and sailors I most respect. Like William Albert Robinson, whose seventy-foot brigantine *Varua* is my favorite boat in all the world. Robinson circumnavigated in a small ketch called *Svaap* in the 1920s, and then designed *Varua*, his "ultimate" ship, with Starling Burgess, and in it he experienced the "ultimate" storm: "Again and again that night, I asked myself why I was there—and had no better answer than that perhaps this was the very thing that had drawn me into this voyage: an unexpressed urge to experience a real Cape Horn gale." Robinson built *Varua* in his

own shipyard in Gloucester, Massachusetts, starting construction in 1939—the same year *Toad* was built—and then sailed it to Tahiti, where he lived for the rest of his life. He wrote about this ship and his life sailing it around the Pacific, and through the Roaring Forties to Chile, in two of my favorite books, *Return to the Sea*, and *To the Great Southern Sea*. But if I take them, what do I leave behind? *Skiffs and Schooners; Boats, Oars and Rowing;* and *Spray*? All by R. D. "Pete" Culler, who learned marlinspike seamanship from a man "who had learned his seamanship under men who had sailed with Nelson." Bill Tilman's *Mischief in Patagonia*? My Knox-Johnston, Moitessier, Crowhurst books? *Sailing Alone Around the World* by Slocum? Chapelle's *Boatbuildling*, and *Yacht Designing and Planning*? . . . My Hiscocks, for fuck's sake? It doesn't matter that I've read them all; they are my library, I refer to them constantly, for reassurance more than anything, to know that this world I've read about and want to be a part of exists, and I feel a chill intimation of a coming loneliness at the thought of leaving them all behind.

I take the Hiscocks, all nine of them; Eric's complete oeuvre, hardbacked, blue cloth, Oxford University Press. They are salt-stained, half-ruined, broken-spined, dust jackets long disintegrated, the foundation of my library—and of who I am, for they describe all I want to do and the world in which I want to do it—and upon them I will build once more from scratch. The rest I hope I can find again.

At 1500 I make another mayday call. No response—until, minutes after I've stopped and gone back to my packing for a new life, a clear static-free voice fills the cabin:

"Ship calling mayday, this is the *Almeria Lykes. Almeria Lykes* responding to mayday, come back."

For all my desperate confidence of being picked up, relief floods me. I think: *Wow, that was fast.*

"Yes, *Almeria Lykes*, this is the sailing yacht *Toad*. I'm at 36°08' north, 53°12' west, and I am sinking. Over."

The voice on the radio, a voice of calm, of authority, tells me

that he is about twenty miles from my position. (He talks in a seigneurial first-person singular: not we, not the ship, but "I am about twenty miles . . .") He is a container ship, on his way from Rotterdam to Galveston, Texas. He asks me how sure I am of the position I have given. Pretty sure, I reply, within a couple of miles—sure that if they come to that position I will see them. The voice responds that he is on his way. He will be there in an hour. He will remain standing by on the air.

I hang up the mike and look around *Toad*'s saloon. After six years, an hour more. After an immeasurable moment I resume packing. I can, of course, take more than these clothes, the Hiscocks, and the grab bag I had ready to take in the dinghy (in fact, I will leave my Neal's yard peanut butter and Gibbon's *Decline and Fall* behind), but already I can see myself afoot in America. I have about $60 and an English Barclaycard Visa with a £100 limit. I will be starting my new life in a Texas bus station. I will have to hump everything, God knows how far, or for how long. I must travel light. I must be ruthless.

I am a sailor. This is how I hope to make my living. So I put my varnished sextant box into the cockpit. Into the sailbag, on top of my irreducible wardrobe, I cram all my charts, my Filofax with my Coast Guard hundred-ton license and my passport, oilskin jacket and pants and seaboots. In go the Hiscocks, camera, exposed film, envelopes of loose photographs, and my logbook of this voyage, the last entry reading:

1500: Mayday call replied to by Almeria Lykes, *a container ship bound for Galveston. Gave him my position and he said he'd be here in an hour.*

My Seiko is on my wrist, and around my neck is my Azorean scrimshaw of *Toad*.

For J., I throw in her five hardback diaries.

On top of them I place the folder containing the novel I've been trying to write. I suspect it's not what I want it to be. I yearn to write something great and wonderful—much better than this novel—but I don't know yet what that might be.

I take my Olivetti up into the cockpit, put it next to the sextant box, look up and see the ship on the horizon. Black and square. It looks like a building. I go below and call him on the radio, tell him I see him, give him his bearing from me—let him work out the reciprocal, I'm too busy.

I go back up into the cockpit and start pumping, partly because I can't stand the sight of so much water below, also because I don't want *Toad* to sink before the ship gets here. I don't know how long it will take the ship to maneuver alongside or how all that will work.

The ship is now about three or four miles away. He calls over the radio to tell me he's spotted me, made visual contact.

I watch it get bigger and bigger, its shape and details growing more definite. It's ugly, slab-sided, tier upon tier of containers— red, gray, blue, rust—stacked high above the black hull along its entire length. Almost no superstructure visible except the bridge at the very front, right up in the bow where it doesn't belong according to all the laws of ship aesthetics as I know them. The closer it gets, growing huger and uglier, the less it looks like a ship. Finally, it has the size and appearance of a mall nearing the end of construction: rectangular, black, and nine hundred feet long, I will learn later this afternoon. Mr. East would hate it, feel it was an abomination. I don't know how to feel. It looks like Armageddon and it's coming to save me.

The ship—ALMERIA LYKES I see on its bow, and LYKES LINES in enormous white three-story letters along the black hull— approaches from windward, leaving us becalmed in a short chop. His voice comes up out of the cabin, from my radio, to tell me that he's going to stop, drift down to me, throw me a line to fasten at *Toad*'s bow. He will then move ahead at his slowest speed, several knots, and we will be pulled in alongside the hull. He will drop a rope ladder, which I am to climb up.

Soon the ship is all I see. It drifts toward us, sideways, blotting out half the visible world. The black hull stretches from horizon to horizon along *Toad*'s starboard side and goes all the way up to the sky.

My hackles rise—no metaphor: the back of my scalp is contracting tightly. This is against all my small-boat sailor's instincts. I should clap on sail and get away from this monster that can mean only one thing to *Toad*: damage. The last time I was on a small boat this close to a larger one was with Bill on *Mary Nell* as the Russian lassoed us and pulled us in and *Mary Nell*'s masts both snapped like dry twigs.

Toad is half turned toward this black wall, now about fifteen feet away. Instinctively, with no thought at all, I dance across the cabin top, over the foredeck, out onto the bowsprit. I stand on the very tip, holding onto the forestay. The black steel plate—pitted, dull, and uneven up close—is closing fast. *Toad*'s angle is all wrong.

I look up for a moment: high above me, peering over the top of the hull, I see a man with long blond hair and a mustache. He's waving. Waving me back.

The ship is a foot away. I stick out my foot now, bracing the other on the bowsprit, to push it off, or push us off. Suddenly this is a collision, that's all I know.

And we collide: the tip of *Toad*'s bowsprit, four inches from my foot, meets the black wall. There's a *crack*—I'm flying through the air, still holding on to the forestay—and then I land back on the cabin top by the mast. The bowsprit is broken, snapped immediately on contact. The forestay, attached to the end of the bowsprit, under tension from the mast and rig, has whipped backward, carrying me with it like Tarzan on a jungle creeper. I land at the mast (which remains upright, held by the inner forestay, which was not set up when the mast fell backward in St. Thomas harbor five years ago). I look at the jagged broken stump of sprit in the bow, and the other piece lying by my foot, and think about how to fix it . . . and then I pull myself away from this thought and push myself toward what must be done.

A shout from above: I look up again and the blond man swings a coil of line right above me, which as I watch turns into a helix as it falls through space and drops onto *Toad*'s foredeck. I fasten the end to the oversize bronze cleat on the foredeck that I took off the Chris Craft lying on the hard in the Lagoon one night years ago.

The small chop, the collision, perhaps even my attempt to push us off have caused us to drift away from the ship's hull. But now the ship begins to move slowly ahead. Tension straightens the line at *Toad*'s bow, and we are pulled forward and in against the black hull. *Toad*'s three-quarter-inch larch planking smacks and bumps against the black steel and I just try not to think about it.

A bright orange rope ladder drops down over the side of the ship astern of us. Someone starts letting out the line holding *Toad* alongside and we are eased back along the hull until we are bobbing and thumping against the ladder. Small, thin lines are dropped down into the cockpit where my bags are packed and ready.

The blond man is now about thirty feet directly above me. I can hear him clearly. He tells me to tie my bags to the small lines. I do this and crewmen haul them up over the side. They are careful with the sextant, keeping it from banging into the steel on the way up. Four items altogether: a sailbag, the sextant, the typewriter, and a Bellingham overnight bag.

"Is that it?" the blond man asks me when they're up and out of sight.

"Yes, I'll be right up." And I go below.

I look around. Apart from the water now at my knees, all looks normal aboard *Toad*. Very neat, just as I like it aboard a small boat crammed with years of collected belongings. The kettle on the stove. It's past teatime.

There remains an hour or two of daylight. I know what I must do. I take the bread knife, bend and crawl into the space behind the galley, where the engine would have been, and cut the one-and-a-half-inch-diameter plastic hose between the cockpit drain and its gate valve through the hull. Water begins to gush in, spouting. *Toad* must sink before dark. So no other yacht will smash into it, water-logged but still floating, and sink with it. Full of love and memories, *Toad* is now an obstruction to safe navigation.

I climb back up into the cockpit, grab the orange polypropylene, and start up the rope ladder. An unreal, dislocating sense of what I am doing, deserting and abandoning the thing I love—a suddenly familiar and reverberating sensation—weighing me down. About a thirty-foot climb.

I'm standing on the ship's high deck. The blond man—he's about six-foot-four, looks like a Viking, or like a young Hulk Hogan—grabs my hand and shakes it, grinning.

"Hey, I'm Dan. How you doing?"

The other crewmen around me are also grinning. They introduce themselves. They are all American. This is an exciting episode in the middle of a monotonous trip for them. They're all thrilled.

I'm not sure what I say, but farther along the deck I see someone casting off the line to *Toad*'s bow. He drops it into the sea.

Dan speaks into a portable VHF he's holding in his hand. A moment later the ship shudders. It begins a long arcing turn around *Toad*, which I find I can't take my eyes off.

I'm walking along the deck behind Dan, who's talking to me, though I have no idea what he's saying. This is just like a dream: I observe, but I am completely detached, disembodied from the scene. We go forward, up steps, into the superstructure below the bridge. Inside we continue up steel stairs.

I'm shown into a stateroom, so vast as to confirm that this is a dream. A double bed, a bathroom en suite. It looks like a motel room, but bigger than most. Windows look out at the sea—I crane my head, but I can't see *Toad*. Dan tells me to make myself comfortable, have a shower, and come up and meet the captain, who's on the bridge, one deck up, whenever I'm ready. The other guys bring in my four items of luggage, all I own in the world. Then they all leave.

Again, I look out the window, but I can't see it. *Toad* is behind us somewhere, to port. I leave my stateroom and run—so, so dreamlike with the uphill roll of the ship against me, holding me back—down a long hallway to a door. Through it, I'm outside, on a wing far above the ocean.

Toad is astern, a quarter of a mile away, maybe, looking not quite itself with its stump bowsprit, and conspicuously low in the water. But it still looks good, the paint and varnish glinting in the low sunlight.

Its bow is pointing straight at Maine.

A Short Weird Cruise
to Galveston

July 30

Captain Frank Johnson is a dead ringer for John Wayne in his later years. Taller than Chief Mate Dan, he must be six-five. His feet appear to be eighteen inches long. He has that barrel-shaped girth the Duke acquired, yet he carries it well. He is not fat. He is every inch a captain. He wears well-pressed khaki pants and shirt. Today, as we chatted on the bridge, he stood by the plate-glass windows forward of the helmsman, ceaselessly scanning the sea as we talked, his eyes creased in a permanent squint from years of keeping such a lookout. Only at mealtimes do his eyes open any wider and I can see then they are pale blue, like a baby's. His face is deeply red from hundreds of tiny burst veins, nearly the color of a boiled lobster, the complexion of a nineteenth century whaling captain who has spent a lifetime on a wind- and salt-swept poop rounding the Horn, but since most of Captain Johnson's years at sea would have been spent inside, latterly on the well-sealed, air-conditioned bridge, this might simply be a rather befitting rosacea. He is a Texan, he speaks well, simply, quietly, and with the timbre of authority I heard so clearly on the radio from over the horizon, for it was he who was the voice of his ship.

Captain Johnson has kindly given me the run of his ship. He has extended to me the courtesy he would show the visiting captain of any other ship, the courtesy he would hope to be shown himself. He doesn't treat me like an irresponsible hippie boat bum he had to fish out of the drink, but has accorded me the respect of one captain for another, and I'm grateful for this. I am allowed on the bridge at any time. I can peer into the radar screens (there are three or four of them), lean over the chart to see our latest position, or watch the seaman at the wheel, which he turns half an inch at a time. Pretty boring after a while. No sails to change, no anxiety.

I accompany Dan, the chief mate, on his daily rounds up and

down the deck and through the capacious hold of this massive ship as he checks the rigging holding the containers down. Inside the ship are whole rafts of containers that are floated into an area of the hold that is partially flooded and then pumped out. This area is open to the stern and you can look out at the Niagara Falls of the wake stretching aft to the horizon. He's taken me into the engine room. It is loud and looks like the inside of the nuclear power station in *The China Syndrome*. He's shown me the crews' quarters, and their saloon, a sort of bland lobby next to the dining room where they can watch videos or find trashy paperbacks.

Dan tells me the crew were impressed by the accuracy of the position I gave them once they learned I had no electronic devices aboard but found my way about by sextant. I was, apparently, right where I had said I was.

My stateroom below the bridge, next to the captain's cabin, is usually reserved for the Lykes Line owners or family members, if they have a hankering for a voyage. There are no other guest facilities aboard the *Almeria Lykes*.

I eat at the captain's table, with Captain Johnson and Chief Mate Dan. Just the three of us. Dan eats quickly, without much talk, and usually excuses himself after eight or ten minutes. The food is well prepared and plentiful, the menu (freshly typed for each meal) unrelievedly American. Steak is available for breakfast, lunch, and supper. Captain Johnson unfailingly eats one of these, about the size and shape of a saddle, rare, every evening. The alternatives are meat loaf; hamburgers; hot dogs; chicken, fried or broiled; and liver. These come with potatoes, baked, roasted, or french fried; a vegetable, salad, with a choice of bottled dressings. There is always pie and ice cream for dessert.

Our orders are taken by Frankie, a woman in her early thirties who is about five-foot-two and weighs about two hundred and fifty pounds. She is very respectful of Captain Johnson and Dan, who grunt their orders in her approximate direction as if she were a drive-thru intercom outside a Burger King. She's extremely solicitous of my welfare. I think she believes I've been languishing in a life raft for weeks. I do appear to have lost weight: my Levi's, which I haven't worn since leaving Horta, now fit like someone else's. Frankie presses dessert on me at every meal, and I have acquiesced so far. I love ice cream, anyway, and it seems to make her day. But after two days of steak, meat loaf, pie, and ice cream, I am bunged up and in as much distress as Robin Knox-Johnston when he thought he was dying of too many steak and kidney puddings. So today I'm back on salad, a baked potato, and no dessert. Frankie is unhappy and won't be consoled.

Captain Johnson and I have had some good sailorly gams over our food. He pooh-poohs the idea of any Bermuda Triangle, but he feels that more shipping grief seems to occur in the five-degree square northwest of Bermuda (outside the putative triangle) than in any other watery place he knows. And he knows why, nothing supernatural to it: the northeast-flowing Gulf Stream widens out there across a considerable area of sea, and over this moves a continual series of weather depressions coming off the U.S. east coast. The strongest winds of these systems blow from the northwest through northeast, against the current in the Stream, creating abnormally steep seas. Add to this a heavy concentration of traffic, of both commercial shipping and pleasure boating, and you have the makings of a statistically accident-prone area.

He tells me that during the winter in this area, rolling container ships routinely "throw" containers. Care can be taken to avoid this, he says, by judicial heavy-weather management—going off route to align a ship more perpendicularly to the seas, as yachts must do at times (much as Bernard Moitessier recommended)—but not all masters will bother to do this, worrying more about schedules than the loss of odd bits of insured cargo. As a small-boat sailor, I'm horrified to hear him tell me that this "routinely" happens. This is every sailor's nightmare, hitting a waterlogged container.

He has also paid me the high compliment of telling me plainly that he respects my endeavor of sailing about on a small boat with only a sextant, tables, and chronometer to guide me. None of his officers, he says, would be able to do as much. They take sextant sights daily from the bridge, but only because they must aboard his ship; and because they have the electronic magic boxes aboard, their sights tend to be untrustworthy. The ability to navigate by sextant and one's instincts, and to manage a boat according to the dictates of sea and sky, he feels, is passing, and I agree with him. He is a real seaman, and I believe he knows what I've been up to, as few others will, and I value his appreciation.

The others aboard, Dan included, believe you have to be nuts to go to sea in a small boat. It's bad enough on the *Almeria Lykes*, they like to say, but on something the size of a container or less, well, you have to be crazy. I don't get very far pointing out that it's really quite safe. They don't believe me.

Ever since I've been aboard, I've been bothered by a sense that I gave up too easily. That I could have done something. I've even thought I might have given up because I wanted the boat to sink, to sever my last link with J. I've thought about this and decided to discount it.

I don't know what else I could have done. At the end, even hove-to, I was unable to sleep and keep ahead of the water coming in; moving at all, more water came in. The sheathing was half off and continuing to delaminate. The hull was becoming as porous as a loosely woven basket. But I keep feeling that someone else might have been able to figure out a solution. I think of Knox-Johnston and his seam repair. Or of Marcel Bardiaux, the Frenchman who circumnavigated in the early fifties—whose book, signed by him for me when I met him in the Azores two years ago, I left aboard *Toad*. (Then almost eighty, he had teeth and a boat made of stainless steel and was wooing an Azorean dentist.) Years before, he had hit a reef in the South Pacific that holed his wooden boat, *Les Quatre Vents*, sinking it—almost. While building it, Bardiaux had filled every spare cubic spot inside his boat with sealed empty cans of air, enough to provide the boat with flotation. He sailed it, virtually sunk, with only the rig and sails sticking up out of the water, for four days until he reached a port, where he hauled out and repaired the hole. Moitessier recommended sawdust immersed in the water close to a leaking seam, which pressure would then carry into the seam, plugging it. I would have needed a barge filled with the waste of a lumberyard. I didn't have a hundred empty sealed tin cans. Perhaps I could have made Bermuda, but only if I'd seen what was coming, how quickly the situation would deteriorate, and headed for there much earlier. It was too late by the time the wind rose, directly from Bermuda, and tore the sheathing off. But still I wonder. And I feel a deep shame. I have an inkling now of why captains might once have gone down with their ships.

I wonder what I am to tell J. about how I lost our boat. And what she will think.

I've been running each day since I've been aboard. This ship actually has a running track: a path painted in nonskid paint around the floor of an empty cargo space in the hull beneath the bridge. Dan says a former chief mate, a runner, painted it during a long voyage. I find I have my running shoes with me, the Nikes I wore for the London marathon back in March, though I have no memory of packing them. I run around and around this dark space inside the ship.

I remembered yesterday that I forgot to pack my father's World War II dog tag, inscribed with his name, serial number, and his thumbprint, which I had been using as a key ring. There were two; David has the other one. I left it in the box above the chart table, with my only key, the one to *Toad*'s companionway hatch padlock.

My stateroom is absurdly comfortable. I take several showers a day in my bathroom. Somebody comes in and cleans when I'm out. There is a telephone beside my bed. Dan told me it's connected to the galley and all I have to do is pick it up to get anything I want delivered to my cabin. I haven't ordered anything yet. I don't want anybody coming into this room while I'm in it. I like being alone in here.

The sense of being in a dream has not worn off at all. I see the ship through a membrane that blocks my feelings. It's like watching a TV documentary: interesting, but remote. At odd moments, talking about the sea with Captain Johnson, who is a warm, kindly man, some quivery emotions have bubbled up inside me, forcing me to bend over my plate or give in to Frankie and eat some ice cream.

It is only during the night, when I wake—and I wake frequently—that I feel I wake from this dream. Then I look around this stateroom and know I'm in the wrong place, and remember with a great lurch what has happened. I used to come up into the cockpit at night and marvel at *Toad* plowing on with no help from me, but I know that it really did need me and I have abandoned it. Days ago now. Far behind. Left it to save my sorry ass. *Toad is gone.*

July 31

I am back in familiar waters: the Bahamas. This morning we passed through "Hole in the Wall," the twenty-odd-mile deepwater gap between the southern tip of Great Abaco Island and the cluster of islands—Royal Island, Russel Island, Spanish Wells—at the north end of Eleuthera. Then we turned right, west, into Northwest Providence Channel, which separates the Berry Islands, where J. and I rode out Hurricane David, and the Abacos. We're now steaming toward Florida.

J. and I sailed this way, through the Northwest Providence Channel, heading east, on all our yacht deliveries from Florida to the Virgins. We always stopped to refuel and sometimes spend the night at Spanish Wells, an island populated by about a thousand white Bahamians named Pinder, descendants of an English loyalist family of that name that fled the American Colonies during the Revolution. When we first arrived at Spanish Wells, we were cleared by Mr. Pinder the immigration officer, and I asked him if his bar, Pinder's Bar, beside the dock, had plenty of cold beer.

"Dunno," said Mr. Pinder. "Never been in there. Don't drink."

"Isn't that your bar?"

"Nope. Dunno the man. No relation to me."

And we found this was the way in Spanish Wells. A thousand blond, pointy-faced Pinders who claimed coincidence rather than relation for the similarity of everyone else's name and physical features.

Another delivery boat was docked beside us, and we ate dinner that night with its crew, at Pinder's Restaurant, up the street from Pinder's Bar. One of these guys, full of beer and crayfish, asked us what we planned to do after dinner. We were going to bed, but we asked him what he was going to do.

"I'm gonna go swing me a Pinder."

I'm not sure what he meant, but I could tell he was looking forward to it.

Once we came through on a Sunday and saw all the Pinders on their way to church. They had brought out family members who normally remained home and indoors during the rest of the week, the Pinders in whom it looked to me as if the genetic soup had become too thin. It reminded me of the John Wyndham book, *The Chrysalids*, set in a Bible-thumping postnuclear world of genetic mutation, where all the two-headed and extra-legged farmyard animals that differed from the proscribed norm were ceremonially slaughtered, and the human equivalents were cast out and sent to a place called the Badlands, from where they made raids on the self-righteous "normal" folk.

I watch from the bridge as we pass Great Isaac Light at the top of the Great Bahama Bank and turn south into the Florida Straits. At 1700 we are south of Miami, close inshore, only a mile off Fowey Rocks Light at the entrance to Biscayne Bay, out of which J. and I sailed in *Toad* bound east across the Atlantic two years ago. I can see people on the beach on Key Biscayne.

I wish Captain Johnson could let me off here. My friend Bennett lives in Coconut Grove, five miles due west. Thom and Beth are up in Fort Lauderdale. But the *Almeria Lykes* is on a schedule as tight as an airplane's. After he stopped to pick me up, Captain Johnson had to radio Galveston to put their booking at the container dock back by three hours.

In these waters we are surrounded by sailboats. And the view from up here is what I imagine it must be like in a zeppelin, vibrating along at about eighteen knots, a hundred and fifty feet or so above the water. I look down on these dinky little boats from the bridge and compare my visual sightings with how they show up on the radar. Radar is clearly better. It is hard to see some of them by eye way down there on the water in the afternoon light. It would be easy to mow them down without knowing it. What a nuisance they are.

The crew are being very careful, though. There is constant radio communication between the bridge and the lookout stationed right in the bow.

Through the twilight we cruise down the Florida Keys, which look beautiful off to starboard with the red sunset behind them. I wonder why J. and I never sailed down here from Miami. We never seemed to have the time.

August 1

All day we cross the Gulf of Mexico. The sky is dull, white, and hot. The sea is flat, a little chop but no swell, which looks odd after so long on the open heaving ocean, and I sense the encircling continent out of sight over the horizon but getting nearer. My short pleasure cruise is almost over. The sense of dream is fading and I'm coming out of the merciful anesthesia that has dulled my thoughts for the last five days. I'm starting to think about what's next, and getting scared.

In the late afternoon the sky clears and turns a pretty blue and we raise the Bolivar Peninsula and Galveston Island on the Texas coast. Barrier islands with houses on them. We steam alongside them for a while, then enter a pass to Galveston Bay.

A pilot comes aboard. On the bridge Captain Johnson stands back while this man, small, neatly trimmed mustache, hair and mustache dyed black, now gives orders to the helmsman. He navigates our floating mall down a narrow waterway. Beach houses pass by very close on our starboard side. Feeling like an alien coming to earth, I look down on passing tableaux of normal earthlings barbecuing and jumping about in their little backyards.

It's almost dark when we reach the container dock, but lights are blazing, illuminating a vast dockyard, cranes on railways, a fleet of waiting trucks. Captain Johnson takes control again here and stands on the bridge wing giving directions into his handheld VHF. The ship comes alongside with the precision and speed of a space station docking.

Unloading begins immediately. The cranes lift containers off the ship and lower them onto the trucks. The noise of a hundred diesels grinding through their gears reverberates up the side of the ship's hull.

An immigration officer comes aboard. He's unconcerned by my

unorthodox entry into the USA. He stamps passports quickly and is gone. Two Coast Guard officers also come aboard, take down the name of my sunken yacht, and go away. There are no searching questions. I might have murdered someone and left a body aboard *Toad* for all anybody knows or seems to care.

I thank Captain Johnson for his hospitality. He wishes me well, kindly—just like the Duke would, with a nod and a crinkly smile; I even hear "Waal, take care of yourself, Pilgrim," although I'm not sure he actually says this. He gives me a solid handshake, and at the last minute I'm overcome with a gulp of emotion and can't say much. He's become my dad in a funny way in the last few days; an older man who has understood my small effort and said, "Well done." But he has already disappeared with agents and paperwork.

I can't find Dan. Frankie gives me the name of a hotel and helps me carry my bags down a gangplank onto the dock—solid unyielding concrete with gravity I've not felt for almost a month—where a number of taxis wait to carry the crew off to Galveston's fleshpots. I thank her. I get into the cab and am driven away. I look at the ship out the back window until it is lost from view.

Through the streets. Red and green traffic lights. Seven-Elevens. Liquor stores. Vagrants on street corners. The cab reeks of smoke and sweat and moves at what appears breakneck speed.

Some stars shine in the evening sky, but, disoriented, I don't recognize them.

Galveston.
And Beyond the Infinite

August 2

I watch the *Today* show and find it difficult to shower and dress. It's hard to pull away and do anything else while it's on. I find myself spending long minutes standing in the middle of the room gaping at the TV. Finally I manage to turn it off, and I call my cousin Poppy in Connecticut.

"You *what?*" she says. "You're *where?*"

I can stay with her as long as I like, forever, she says. And her brother Matt, who is also a best friend, lives in Manhattan. So I will head there. Maybe I'll go to Maine later, but I saw myself there on a boat. Without a boat Maine will be a room ashore like any other place. Beyond Poppy's, I have no idea yet what I'll do. Get some work, somewhere. See what things look like when I've come down, returned to earth, which I don't feel I've done yet.

"So, wait, what was your trip like?" Poppy asks.

"Well . . . I'll tell you when I get there."

The hotel accepts my Barclaycard. I take a taxi to the bus station. My Barclaycard also buys me a bus ticket to New York City. That's more than £100 now. I'm in debt already, the proper way to begin life in America.

I think: *How will I ever tell Poppy and Matt what my trip was like? How do I explain it?*

I change buses in Houston. I find I can just carry everything at once as I move through the bus station. I don't want to leave half my bags in one place and relay them to another. I'm worried about theft.

All I need is a shopping cart. That would hold everything nicely, and I'd fit the homeless paradigm to a T. I am now worse off than Wilfred in Mylor, my former benchmark of how far I feared I might fall. I can be reduced no further unless I begin to lose body parts.

Reminds me of the joke about the guy who's just a head and torso in a hospital bed, and is upset because he's about to lose a tooth.

I've read enough to know I could look upon my new situation as a spiritual opportunity: as divested of material burden as a Brahman mendicant, I am now free. I could wander off to a mountaintop, or to a New Age Disneyland like Sedona, Arizona, and travel inward, a journey farther and more difficult than going to Burma. This unencumbered state often seems appealing to the mass of men leading lives of quiet desperation, but standing in a Trailways bus station with my poor bundles, it makes me want a car, and money for gas, and, somewhere down the lonesome road, a Whopper. I'm not ready to pass over the razor's edge and commence the greatest journey.

The bus out of Houston takes me east along Interstate 10. One part of America looks so like another. I've never been here before, but it all looks familiar.

I keep coming back to America, and I wonder why. Perhaps because I was removed at an early age. I was resentful of this later on, in my Dickensian boarding school, where I was beaten with a bamboo cane, where there were no girls, and where I listened to the Beach Boys and heard what I was missing in the good ole USA. I came back for college, but didn't find it. Then later, again and again, but I always fled back to England, defeated, hating America because it wasn't what I thought it should be.

Now here it is rolling by so familiarly out the window, and here I am again, with just my sextant, my scrimshaw, and my Hiscocks. And my blazer, which I forgot to hang up in the shower this morning. This isn't how I wanted to tackle America again. Life on a boat, the separateness, has been my protection. But perhaps it has isolated me too—made me the thing I feared being: a satellite as unattached as Klaus in Horta. Maybe it will now be a good thing that I won't be able to sail away as soon as the urge takes me.

I look out the window and I'm full of hope. I hope to find work

I like. I hope to meet a woman I like who likes me. I hope to write something good. I hope somehow to get another boat.

I think of lines by T. S. Eliot, from *Little Gidding*, in a book that sank with *Toad*:

> *We shall not cease from exploration*
> *And the end of all our exploring*
> *Will be to arrive where we started*
> *And know the place for the first time.*

However, by late afternoon, somewhere in Louisiana, I am getting the mother of all backaches. Living in the never-still *Toad*, even aboard the gentle *Almeria Lykes*, I have experienced nothing like this fiendish bus seat since perhaps the last time I visited a dentist. I get out whenever we stop, and bend and stretch, but it doesn't seem to help. I'm getting a terrible headache too. Noise is bothering me: the grinding of the bus, the raucous twangy braying of people in bus stations. It may be English they're speaking, but it's as arcane as the dockers' babble that came up over the *Caronia*'s side in Southampton in 1959. Despite my earlier hopeful embrace of America, it's beginning to look like a nightmare out there. I feel myself withdrawing into a familiar solipsism.

For supper I eat an apple pie, apparently made in New Jersey, which I buy wrapped in cellophane from a snack machine in Mississippi.

As the bus hums through the dark, I look out the window at the flat landscape and think of the sea. And then of *Toad*, and the whole thought of it comes over me in a rush. I think again of all J. and I did to that boat, how we rebuilt it, renamed it and gave it its last incarnation, where it took us, and finally where it took me.

Now for the first time I begin to think about what *Toad* has done for me, and suddenly it becomes clear. *Toad* showed me that I could use scavenged inner-tube rubber to replace the diaphragm on a galley pump. That I could be a carpenter if I needed to be, or a navigator; that I could sleep for no longer than thirty minutes at a time for weeks on end. That after disgracing myself years ago in a Bristol Channel gale, I could go back to sea alone and acquit myself well. For most of the last forty days, *Toad* and I flew across the sea together as sleekly and happily as partners in a fairy tale: a boy riding on a magic dolphin. Through my shame and grief I find I'm proud of our fine voyage. The ending was simply how it finished, not the voyage itself.

What I will do now is find my way back to sea.